CISTERCIAN STUDIES SERIES: NUMBER FIFTY-THREE

Irénée Hausherr

# PENTHOS

# THE DOCTRINE OF COMPUNCTION

TRANSLATED BY
Anselm Hufstader, OSB

CISTERCIAN STUDIES SERIES: NUMBER FIFTY-THREE

# PENTHOS

## IN THE CHRISTIAN EAST

*by Irénée Hausherr*, SJ

CISTERCIAN PUBLICATIONS, INC.
Kalamazoo, Michigan
1982

A translation of *Penthos: La doctrine de componction dans l'Orient Chrétien. Orientalia Christiana Analecta,* 132. Rome, 1944.


Available in Britain and Europe through
A. R. Mowbray & Co Ltd  St Thomas House
Becket Street  Oxford OX1 1SJ

Library of Congress Cataloguing-in-Publication Data

Hausherr, Irénée, 1891-
    Penthos: the doctrine of compunction in the Christian East.

    (Cistercian studies series ; no. 53)
    Translation of: Penthos.
    1. Repentance—History of doctrines.
2. Eastern churches—Doctrinal and controversial works.
I. Title.  II. Series.
BT800.H3813    234'.5    82-1258
ISBN 0-87907-853-7        AACR2

Typeset by Gale Akins, Kalamazoo
Printed in the United States of America

# TABLE OF CONTENTS

# TRANSLATOR'S NOTE

THE TRANSLATION OF THIS STUDY, one too little known in the English-speaking world, has presented one major difficulty. Much of the text consists of Father Hausherr's translations of original sources. The task of finding all these passages and having them translated appeared insurmontable. Remembering Chesterton's maxim that if a thing is worth doing at all it is worth doing badly, I have, for the most part, translated translations. The exceptions to this, notably Benedicta Ward's new translation of the Alphabetic Sayings, have been noted. For the rest, I can only hope that the violence done to the originals is not too extensive, and that the references will stimulate dissatisfied readers to their own pursuit of the sources, and beyond.

The references themselves have, however, constituted a second difficulty. While being a work of great erudition, Father Hausherr's text does not always provide bibliographical information to satisfy today's standards. Details, such as place and date of an edition, have been added wherever possible, but some footnotes are still imprecise. Many of Father Hausherr's sources have appeared in new editions and translations since his book appeared. Although there is some acknowledgement of this, many of the older references must be allowed to stand.

A.H.

# TRANSLATOR'S PREFACE

> . . . a purely temporal, and, for all I know, what
> the monks back at the ironworks would have called
> a carnal feeling, but a source of continual comfort
> to me. Let them go their way and let me go mine.
>                   Hilaire Belloc, *The Path to Rome*

It matters little that Belloc was speaking of the (purely
human) pleasure attached to attendance at morning Mass. His
thoughts about the monks back at the ironworks would,
I fear, only have been confirmed had he seen Father
Hausherr's study of monastic compunction. Nor would
Belloc be alone. How many other readers will find *penthos*
a morbid theme, at best a curiosity of the remote christian
past? 'Let them go their way and let me go mine.'

It is not, in fact, my purpose to recommend the revival of
an old way. Religious sensibility and its expressions live in
the past. Yet *penthos* is not so strange that we should walk
away from it. It is certainly not morbid and, if Father
Hausherr is right, it is in *some* form essential to the joy of
the Resurrection. My own feeling is that, far from being
outdated, the teaching of the Fathers on compunction has a
very special urgency for Christians of our era. The very
strangeness of their words may serve to throw new light on
our own experience. Should we judge the past by the present
or the present by the past? In either case, we should avoid
assuming too much, especially about ourselves.

It is with a view to promoting this dialogue that I offer
some of my own reflections on the present, prompted by
Father Hausherr's treatment of the past.

## I.

The place to begin is with the largely unquestioned assumption of our culture that guilt is a psychological misfortune from which an enlightened education or, if necessary, treatment can deliver innocent sufferers. We have come to see moral codes of the recent past as excessively burdensome and restricting, nowhere more so than in conservative religious milieux, where God, clergymen, and parents all conspired to oppress the growing child. The sinister priest, 'the man who invented sin', has become a stock character in our moral mythology. Guilt, says the myth, has been imposed on us by society, ultimately as a form of control. Outward order is achieved at the price of inner destruction. The counter-myth reaffirms the natural goodness of man and the value of his spontaneous self-expression. It desires that society replace moral absolutes with more modest expectations of successful role-playing and self-fulfillment, above all the latter. Self-fulfillment is another word for innocence, which is the opposite of guilt.[1]

Since the myth saw guilt as coming from a stern lawgiving God, that God had to die. This, of course, was seen to, and it is no longer a secret that the ethos of living without guilt is also that of atheism. That all things would be permitted if God did not exist was a prospect which alarmed Dostoievsky. Later it alarmed Camus as well, who protested in *The Rebel* that, since God does not exist, man must be even stricter with himself than God would have been. It has not worked out that way. One would like to invite the advocates of the new permissiveness to tell us how, since they have had their way, men are truly freer and more happy.

In one of his last writings, *Sincerity and Authenticity*, Lionel Trilling touched the heart of this matter. Speaking of 'authenticity' as a sense of personal reality, he noticed the devastating psychological effects on man of the removal of ethical absolutes, occasioned by the celebrated death of God.

The sense of no limits, of free floating in a viscous goo, with no real reason *why* one should do one thing rather than another, is not healthy. Trilling associates this with the demise of narrative literature, the loss of any sense of the past. Turning to the question of guilt, Trilling notices the important development of Freud's thought from an earlier position, where repression was seen as learned, to that of *Civilization and its Discontents,* where the self-persecuting super-ego is seen as equally unconscious as the libido. The point is that Freud, of all people, rejected the myth of guilt as imposed on us by society and moved to the starker reality of guilt as imposed on us by ourselves. If this is the case, he admitted, man's suffering may be irremediable, and Trilling suggests that such a conclusion may be the necessary price to pay if we are to avoid lives totally devoid of meaning. The image of the painfully dying Freud, outrated at the well-meaning doctor who had given him a sedative and demanding *by what right* this had been done, is symbolic of the moralist's insistence on the sense of reality which could only be achieved through the experience, however painful, of limits.

Freud, of course, remained an atheist, leaving Trilling and others to speculate on the degree to which the severe and punishing super-ego resembles that severe and punishing Jahweh which Freud had earlier abandoned. A more recent psychiatrist, Karl Menninger, has been somewhat more theologically explicit in his *Whatever Became of Sin?* Unaccountability is unhealthy. Unhealthier still is a value-system in which there is no place to rest our burden of guilt. Liberal thought tried to eliminate guilt after eliminating its divine source, such as it was imagined to be. Could it be that it only removed man's faith in the real God, steadfast in mercy and loving-kindness, who alone is powerful to forgive and remove the guilt which man alone incurs?

## II.

*Penthos* is not a book about guilt or sin. It presupposes these facts as those of the human condition, and studies the christian phenomenon of weeping for one's sins. The key text is the second Beatitude: Blessed—that is, happy—are those who weep. For the ancient monks, unhappiness was the lot of those with dry eyes and a cold heart. Unending happiness was perpetual compunction. Before *penthos* can continue it must begin, and the initial point of compunction is *metanoia,* the moment when the heart is pierced. Scripture is full of these liberating shocks of repentance, from David's 'I have sinned' (2 Sam 12:13) to the hearers of Saint Peter who were 'cut to the heart' at the realization that they had crucified the Lord, repented, and were baptized (Ac 2:37). *Metanoia,* or repentance, is that moment of grace when the truth about ourselves and God strikes us, pierces the heart, and makes a new life possible.

The fact that this moment of grace is little known in our world in no way diminishes its importance—quite the contrary. In T.S. Eliot's *The Cocktail Party,* Celia's conversion begins with a sense of sin.

> REILLY. You suffer from a sense of sin, Miss
> Coplestone? This is most unusual.
> CELIA.                     It seemed to *me* abnormal.
> She has no way of accounting for the origin of this idea.
> Well, my bringing up was pretty conventional—
> I had always been taught to disbelieve in sin.
> Oh, I don't mean that it was ever mentioned!
> But anything wrong, from our point of view,
> Was either bad form, or was psychological.
> She finally says how she feels.
> It's not the feeling of anything I've ever *done,*
> Which I might get away from, or of anything in me
> I could get rid of—but of emptiness, of failure

> Towards someone, or something, outside of myself;
> And I feel I must . . . *atone*—is that the word?
> Can you treat a patient for such a state of mind?

This moment is the prelude to Celia's turning from an empty life to one of heroic sanctity, ultimately to a martyr's death.

If compunction really is the threshold of conversion, then it cannot be the exclusive property of Christians. Albert Camus' *The Fall* should be read as a classic expression of non-christian compunction. There is no mistaking the situation. Its hero is a prophet, Jean–Baptiste Clamence (John–Baptist *clamans*) with nowhere to point, 'an empty prophet for bad times, Elijah with no Messiah'. At first a successful lawyer, a man of vaulting ego and self-nourishing virtues, he had suddenly begun to discover cracks in his edifice. His refusal to save a woman from drowning revealed to him his unwillingness to do good except on his own terms. With that the fall began, and continued until Clamence ended in a dive in Amsterdam, whose concentric canals suggest the circles of Dante's hell, perpetually confessing his sins to lead others to repentance—a judge-penitent. This third and last novel of Camus represents no small evolution of his thought from *The Stranger,* from which all moral values are almost totally absent, and *The Plague,* in which evil has been identified and must be fought, but is still totally *other* than the human consciousness. In *The Fall,* evil is what we have done and are. As he turns from repentance to judgement, the unrelenting Clamence depicts us as maintaining our own innocence (for this is our primary goal) only by fastening guilt on others. The pathos of it all is that, for the atheist Camus, there is no source of forgiveness. A beggar had once grasped his hand and said, 'Ah, monsieur, it is not that one is bad, but one loses the light'. 'Yes,' adds Clamence, 'we have lost the light, the mornings, the holy innocence of him who forgives himself'. At that, we can only wonder what the fourth novel would have brought had not Camus' life ended soon after *The Fall* in an automobile accident.

I feel that the prophetic heroes of Father Hausherr's book, crying out from their desert a message of divine love, would have perfectly understood Celia and Clamence, and so many others of us seeking a place to leave our self-righteousness.

## III.

Even if we admit the importance of compunction today, there remains the problem of our religious attitudes. Those described in *Penthos* will, I think, appear very remote to the majority of readers. Let us avoid revivals! All of them. The danger of trying to reconstruct Scete is less real than that of a call to a new Puritanism, or even a new legalism. We must not confuse fear and scruples with contrition and tears. Hausherr points out that the multiplication of confessions did not necessarily enhance the spirit of repentance. One wonders what he would say about today's decline in the practice of this sacrament. Perhaps both trends are equally unfavorable to a spirit of repentance, wherein may lie the link between them. Yet the question—'where to go from here?'—remains.

It is always easier to criticize than to construct. Our churches are decked with banners which say 'Joy' and 'Peace'. At the same time, the vocabulary of liberal humanism—'self-fulfillment' and the like—has crept into our religious language and from there into our liturgy. Yet who would claim that this proliferation of symbols for human happiness denotes any significantly corresponding realities in our congregations? Is it true, once again, that we forget to speak of what we have, but talk incessantly of what we long for? Many Christians do indeed seek the gifts of the Spirit, in their outward manifestations as charisms, and inwardly in techniques of prayer. We seem to be aiming high, but falling short. Have we forgotten something?

One of the older fathers of my community used to say

that our age surpassed all others in unreflectiveness, in
a lack of self-awareness. I did not agree then, thinking that
we were if anything too self-conscious. Now I think he was
right. Self-consciousness is not what he meant; that is a concern for how we appear. He meant a concern for what we
are, examination not of our image but of our conscience.
One of the best things a book like Father Hausherr's can do
for us is to disturb us, to force us, through confrontation
with the past, to reflect on ourselves. Are we so sure that
our ways are right, that our joy is authentic? Has our
experience of God been mediated by what others have told
us it should be, or have we been 'cut to the heart', that we
may experience God for ourselves? Have we sought gifts from
God with a view to expanding our personalities without also
asking for limits, that we may know his will? The ultimate
issue—his will or ours—is worked out in our conscience.
'Work out your salvation with fear and trembling,' says
Saint Paul, perhaps thinking of all the dangerous possibilities of self-deception.

The question of religious attitude is, finally, no different
from the question put alike to catechumens and postulants:
'What do you seek?' Let each one answer for himself. Shall
we say, 'Salvation'? *Penthos* urges that we say precisely that,
asking it from God and leaving the further gifts to his good
pleasure. Saint Benedict says the same:

> Daily in one's prayer, with tears and sighs, to
> confess one's past sins to God.
> To amend those sins for the future.
> Not to fulfil the desires of the flesh.
> To hate one's own will . . .
> Not to wish to be called holy before one is
> holy; but first to be holy, that one may more truly
> be called so.

Solemnity of Saint Benedict                              A.H.
11.vii.78

# INTRODUCTION

*The joy of the resurrection is the fundamental characteristic of the Ortho-dox Church's world-view.*

N. Arseniev[1]

*Truly you are blessed, Abba Arsenius, for you wept for yourself in this world!*

Abba Poemen[2]

THE READER IS WARNED not to see in this juxta-position of quotations any intention of setting Monsieur Arseniev against his namesake, Saint Arse-nius. Light springs from contrasts. The seemingly irreconcilable helps us to grasp the fullness of truth. The boundless riches of the Word cannot be confined in one sentence. The most grandiose perspectives are only mirages if our gaze rests on the horizon without seeing, at least with a rapid glance, what lies between. On a beautiful July day, standing by Lake Geneva, you may enjoy the view of Mont Blanc in its majestic splendor. If, like little children, you knew nothing of geography, you might stretch out your hand to touch this far-off whiteness, so close does it seem. Yet it is one hundred kilometres away as the crow flies. For poor hikers like ourselves, how many ups and downs, snow drifts and crevasses, weariness and toil! Children and old men would be foolish to undertake the trip. Only a healthy adult can attempt with any chance of success what a deceptive glance made seem so easy.

'The summit of the spiritual mountain is difficult to

1

reach.'[3] *Mons excelsus,* Tabor, the glorious transfiguration,
the joy of the resurrection. No-one indeed knows this better
than Arseniev, who was 'instructed at the feet of Gamaliel in
the exact knowledge of the law of his fathers', that is, the
fathers of the Eastern Church who are, for the most part,
fathers of the universal Church. His is the pleasant duty of
stirring up a desire for the heights; others will take on the
rugged task of an alpine guide. Let them see to the details of
the expedition, let them calculate to the ounce the weight
and durability of the equipment. The guides owe their
knowledge to their own experience and to the stories of the
elders, the *Apophthegmata Patrum,* the *Verba Seniorum.*

For lack of personal experience, I propose that you listen
to the teachings of the elders concerning one of the qualities
most necessary to the spiritual mountain climber. In Greek
they call it *penthos.* Yet it is not a Greek idea, nor even
Byzantine; it is found under various names (which I will
spare you) in all the languages spoken by Eastern Christians.
Suffice it to recall the Latin terms of the *Verba Seniorum:*
*dolor,* or *luctus.*

# I

## PENTHOS

ΠΈΝΘΟΣ the etymologists tell us, is of the same root as πάθος. Hesychius in his *Lexicon* explains it by συμφορά, θρῆνος, λύπη. It could therefore mean any sort of affliction. The meaning has in fact been specialized in the sense of 'mourning'. '*Luctus, moeror ex morte propinquorum vel amicorum,*' says the *Thesaurus* of Henri Estienne, who adds, '*In prosa pro luctu tantum usurpatum invenio.*' On the other hand: '*Generaliter pro quovis moerore capitur apud poetas.*' There is no trace in all of this of any religious meaning.[2]

Three possible meanings result: 1. Mourning for relatives or friends; 2. Sadness over any mishap; 3. Lamentation for a dead god. What do the Fathers think of these?

1. *Mourning for relatives or friends.* 'A monk was told of the death of his father. "Stop blaspheming," he replied, "my father is immortal".'[3] Saint John Chrysostom, who preached not only for monks, never tired of repeating the lesson learned from Saint Paul: let us not weep for the dead simply because they are dead! This is as unreasonable as it is useless, even philosophically speaking. The Stoics were not mistaken when they placed death among things indifferent.[4] Sometimes mourning is justified by its happy outcome, but not in this case! For Christians worthy of the name, death is birth into true life. At the burial of Caesarius, the brother of Saint Gregory Nazianzen, their mother wore festive clothes.[5] If the cerebral indifference of the Stoic is not enough to console the heart (Chrysostom reminds us that professional

3

mourners made a good living), christian faith will overcome
this sadness in the joy of the resurrection. Because Christ has
conquered death, Christians must not be saddened as are
those who have no hope. The πένθος preached by the Fathers
has nothing to do with this sort of mourning.

2. *Sadness over any mishap.* It follows from this that the
Christian will easily put up with less serious losses. The
*Verba Seniorum* has a chapter entitled, 'The monk must not
be in the least saddened if he happens to lose something'.[6]
Two stories—and there are many others in the *Apophthegmata Patrum*—lend support to this maxim. Like Saint Macarius, Abba Euprepios lends a hand to robbers he has
discovered raiding his cell. Then he runs after them to take
them a stick they had left behind.

'He who loves the world loves occasions of falling. Therefore if we happen to lose something, we must accept this
with joy and gratitude, realizing that we have been set free
from care.'[7] Saint Barsanuphius had learned this teaching
well. A scrupulous monk wrote to him, 'Whenever I suffer
a loss, and my heart is not saddened, my thought tells me
that this is barbarity, that we should on the one hand be
saddened, but at the same time give thanks. Is this suggestion
a good one?' The great old man replies, 'One must absolutely
not be saddened by anything in this world.'[8] This is clear
enough in any case, for sadness figures in the catalogue of the
eight evil thoughts or capital sins. We should never make the
disastrous mistake of confusing the fruit of grace, πένθος,
with the seed of hell, λύπη. Saint Paul, it is true, uses the
latter word in a virtuous sense (2 Cor 7:10), but the ascetics
prefer to give another name to the sadness which is of God, so
great a horror have they of the sadness which is of the
world. To know with what thoroughness they hunted down
this vice, one has only to read the chapter which Evagrius
devotes to the subject in his *Antirrheticon,* where he lists
seventy-seven varieties of sadness, and as many scriptural
reflections enabling us to surmount them.[9] Such are the

changes rung on the stern theme of Saint Barsanuphius.

And there is more: not only should nothing in this world grieve us, but neither, it seems, should anything in the next. Of these seventy-seven paragraphs, the great majority deal with causes which some would call supernatural: fear of demons and of the struggles they cause us, of our own weakness in withstanding them, of the tortures to which they subject the monk, and then discouragement at the remembrance of past sins, or at the thought of being abandoned by God and his angels. Chapter XI of the *Verba Seniorum* is entitled, *Contra spiritum tristitiae qui desperationem facit.* No, πένθος does not flourish in a feeble soul or a cowardly heart.

Still less can it prosper among the lazy. The direct opposite of *penthos* is *accedia,* which dries up the source of tears and drives one to seek out distractions which are fatal to recollection. 'The spirit of accedia drives away tears; the spirit of sadness ruins prayer [for] prayer is a result of joy and gratitude,' and it begins with πένθος.[10] Πένθος and λύπη go in diametrically opposed directions: the first toward the summits of union with God, the second toward the abyss of despair. *Accedia* 'softens and weakens the soul, even destroys it with bitterness by consuming its vigor.'[11] It whispers plans of escape, ways of avoiding the spectacle of its own psychological degradation, while πένθος turns us toward ourselves with the certitude of finding the kingdom of God within. Πένθος is born from ambitious desire in a manly soul. This was the gist of a *fervorino* I once heard a young monk of Iviron giving to a compatriot who had just returned from America: the amusements of the world can never fill the void in a heart empty of God; true joy is what we possess! He was so serious, this little monk with the flowing beard. A superficial observer might have called him and most of his confrères gloomy men. And yet he spoke of happiness with such conviction that he seemed to be winning the American traveller over with his eloquence.

3. *Lamentation for a dead god.* Is there any question of 'sacred mourning'? Could these ascetics be weeping over the death of Christ, as the women of Byblos wept over Adonis? Such an idea tempted Reitzenstein, who would no doubt have referred to the *Apostolic Constitutions* VII.23. In this ancient document we do, indeed, find in no uncertain terms the expression 'mourning for the Lord'.[12] The text is there to justify fasting on a single Saturday of the year, the day 'when the Creator goes below the earth'. Fasting, though, is not compunction. The latter must be perpetual, forbidden by no season, whereas fasting may be limited to Wednesdays and Fridays, and is forbidden on Saturdays (except Holy Saturday) and Sundays. Moreover, the *Apostolic Constitutions* explicitly forbid mourning for Christ: 'For those who do not believe in the Saviour, he is dead, since the hope they have in him is dead; but for you who believe, our Lord and Redeemer has risen, for the hope that you have in him is immortal and lives forever.' It is the Jews who weep for their Messiah: 'Therefore they weep over God, over the Christ who suffered, and with respect to God our Saviour they weep over themselves and their downfall.'[13]

In other words, weeping for Christ is not christian. Monastic *penthos* will never be found related to the death of Christ. In fact, the very thought of Christ is absent from *penthos*—too much so, it might be thought, if one did not know that every virtue, every effort toward perfection, has as its ultimate incentive the love of God. Devotion to the Saviour's passion does not include those outward forms so familiar to us from a later age. It is enough for the moment to have pointed this out. The subject deserves a separate treatment, but that would carry us too far from our subject.

# II

## CATANYXIS

BEFORE WE BEGIN, there is still one more bit of lexicography to be done. A synonym, or nearly that, of *penthos* is *catanyxis* (κατάνυξις). While the first term obviously comes from the second beatitude (Mt 5:4), the second does not appear to have a scriptural origin.[1] In the only passage in the New Testament where it occurs (Rm 11:8, citing Is 29:10), it has a clearly unfavorable sense: 'For the Lord has poured out upon you a spirit of *deep sleep,* and has closed your eyes, the prophets, and covered your heads, the seers'. (RSV; Vg: *spiritum compunctionis*). When Cassian recommends *compunctio* or Saint Chrysostom κατάνυξις, there can be no thought of allusion to this verse. Yet Bailly's *Dictionary* refers to it for the sense of 'compunction, that is regret that is felt in the depths of the heart for having sinned'. A second reference to *LXX* Ps 29:15[2] is no better. If Ps 59:5 is read first, then the expression οἶνος κατανύξεως will be seen to have a quite inappropriate meaning. These are the only two occurences of this noun in the Old and New Testaments. More frequent is the verb κατανύσσω or, better, κατανυγῆναι, always in the passive, whether aorist or perfect. Thus, Gn 27:38: κατενυχθέντος Ἰσάακ. (Isaac is moved by the lamentations of Esau); Gn 34:7: κα]ενύχθησαν ἄν δρες (these men were outraged at the dishonor inflicted on Dinah). This same meaning of strong emotion is found still elsewhere. Sometimes the word seems rather to indicate a consequence of this feeling. For example, 1 K 20:27, 29: κατενύγη

7

ἀπὸ προσώπου τοῦ κυρίου (Ahab humiliated himself before
the Lord, he went weeping, rent his garments, put on sackcloth and fasted). In Lv 10:3, κατενύχθη 'Ααρών corresponds
to *tacuit Aaron* in the Vulgate. Aaron kept silence, stricken
from learning of the death of his sons. This sense of keeping
silence, or desisting, is found again in the Psalms (4:5, 29:13,
34:15), and has been kept by Hesychius in a gloss of his
*Lexicon: κατάνυξις = ἡσυχία ἢ λύπη.* Once the concept of
ascetic compunction was established, however, it was natural
to see it in such texts as *in cubilibus vestris compungimini*
(Ps 4:5). Special notice should be taken of Ps 108:16: 'He
has persecuted the helpless, the destitute, and those stricken
in heart'. (κατανενυγμένον τῇ καρδίᾳ). This expression is
found again in Ac 2:37: 'When they heard this, they were
cut to the heart (κατενύγησαν τὴν καρδίαν) and said,
"Brothers, what must we do?" '

Κατάνυξις is thus a sudden shock, an emotion which
plants deep in the soul a feeling, an attitude, or a resolution.
Suidas, after citing the verse of Isaiah quoted by Saint Paul,
adds a passage from Saint John Chrysostom, given here in
fuller context:

> He intends to speak of a troublesome *habitus* of
> the soul, one without hope of remedy or change.
> In another place David says, 'May my glory sing
> to you, and I will not cease'. (οὐ μὴ κατανυγῶ,
> Ps 29:13). For just as he who is κατανενυγμένος
> in holiness does not readily depart from it, so he
> who is κατανυγεὶς in wickedness cannot easily
> change. Κατανυγῆναι is, precisely, then, to be
> fixed or nailed to something. It is thus to show
> that their dispositions are incurable, difficult to
> change, that Saint Paul has spoken of the spirit of
> compunction.[3]

Henceforth the connection between *catanyxis* and *penthos*
is clear. The former (naming an action) denotes a shock

which comes from without; the latter is the psychological reaction. Abba Timothy, a priest, was sent by Saint Poemen to Alexandria to try to convert a fallen woman. 'When the woman saw him and heard the word of God from him, κατενύγη καὶ ἔκλαυσεν, she was filled with compunction and said to him weeping, "From today forward I shall cling to God . . . " ' [4] The shock can also come from within, from meditation. 'Abba Hyperychios said, "The monk labors night and day in vigils and unceasing prayer; *pungens autem cor suum producit lacrimas*—by piercing his heart he produces tears".'[5]

The shock can, of course, have other immediate effects than tears. Euprepios, having asked for and obtained a salutary word, κατάνυγεὶς ἔβαλε μετάνοιαν: 'Filled with compunction at this saying, he made a prostration, saying, "I have read many books before, but never have I received such teaching".'[6] Then there is this pleasant story:

> A brother sought out an old man and said to him, 'What shall I do? I am tortured by pride.' The old man said to him, 'You are right to be proud, since it is you who made heaven and earth.' At this the brother κατανυγείς, touched with compunction, made a prostration and said, 'Forgive me, I have done nothing of the sort'.[7]

In practice, however, compunction, mourning and tears go together so much that they are, through metonymy, virtual equivalents. Saint Barsanuphius, replying to Saint Dorotheos, simply remarks that compunction is the cause and tears the effect:

> How can you conserve penthos, when you must come and go and occupy yourself with business? Is there a penthos without tears? It is not 'mourning.' Even if you move among men you will have compunction if you master your own will and pay no attention to the misdeeds of men. If you do this, your thoughts will be recollected, and thus

they will engender godly mourning in your heart,
and the mourning of tears.[8]

For the Latins, since Cassian, *compunctio* has prevailed over
*luctus,* which had been used in the *Verba Seniorum.* Cassian
is a disciple of Chrysostom, who wrote a special treatise on
catanyxis. Even among the Greeks it is the latter word which
has dominated, without however eliminating penthos, so
much used in the ancient documents. There are in the
'catanyctic' troparia, canons and kathismata, all designed to
produce compunction.[9] Such prayers were gathered together,
and finally these collections were called *catanyxis.*

# III

## SOURCES OF *PENTHOS*

THE EASTERN WRITINGS on compunction are many. It will be enough here to point out at least a few of them to show the continuity of the doctrine through the christian centuries.

Clement of Alexandria recommends that we abstain 'from excessive laughter and from tears'.[1] He read this much in Plato,[2] and proposed to reconcile it with the Gospel. He did this by adding to δακρύων the adjective ὑπερμέτρων: tears which exceed limits. He knew, nevertheless, that tears mean repentance,[3] and that 'to weep and wear mourning for justice's sake is to bear witness to the most wonderful Law, that it is good'.[4] He had his own way of accounting for the Beatitude concerning those who weep.[5] Not that he was the apostle of *penthos;* he was too speculative for that. Soon a saint would be heard to declare that excessive application to theological books dries up compunction. As for κατάνυξις, Clement knew nothing of it. No amount of sympathy for him will allow us to see here the ideal of the christian way of life.

It has been said that Origen is more christian than Clement. Is he in fact more favorable to compunction? As a commentator on Jeremiah, he could scarcely fail to be. 'Prolonged prayer and intensity of tears incline God to mercy,' he declared.[6] In the nineteenth homily *On Jeremiah* he developed the idea that a preacher should use his eloquence to bring his hearers 'to mourning, to weeping and to tears'. The road is rough and narrow; no-one can walk it without hardship. Yet it alone leads to life; 'only weeping leads to

blessed laughter'. He apologized for bringing up such disagreeable and bitter thoughts, but did not the prophet say it
himself: *amaro verbo meo ridebo*?[7] We do not know how he
interpreted the second beatitude (the third in the Vulgate);
this part of his commentary on Matthew has been lost. But
he did say this: 'Jesus wished to show in himself all the
beatitudes, for he also said, "Blessed are those who weep,"
and he himself wept in order to lay the foundation of this
beatitude as well.' As for the Jerusalem over which Jesus
wept, it is ourselves, all the more to be wept over since we
have sinned 'after the mysteries of truth, after the preaching
of the Gospel, after the doctrine of the Church, after the
sight of the sacraments'.[8] More christian than Clement,
less lost in hellenic speculation, Origen would not have cared
to transcribe the platonic condemnation of tears, even with a
corrective. Yet still it is not he who is to be the great master
of compunction.

  I can do no better here than give some lines from
W. Völker's admirable exposition of Origen's doctrine of the
struggle against sin, in which he portrays the Alexandrian as
the first great preacher of compunction:

> The seriousness with which Origen considers sin is
> shown in his homilies on Jeremiah, where he
> declares that every wrong act leaves on the soul an
> indelible mark ($τύπος$) to be made manifest on the
> day of judgement.[9] His knowledge of the interior
> life is further evident in a homily on the Psalms,
> where he speaks of committed sins returning to
> life in the heart, seeing in this reviviscence their
> true punishment.[10] Now if sin remains alive it
> must, long after the sinful act, exercise a depress-
> ing influence on a man, taking away his *parrhēsia*,[11]
> and thereby widening the gulf between the sinner
> and God. The traces left in man by sin show
> themselves finally in the sense of a universal
> consciousness of sin, a feeling which Origen often

expressed in his homilies and which originated in quite a different area of his thought . . . . As far as he is concerned, Origen knows that from the soil of his soul rises up a 'thick wood' (μύρια ξύλα) which must first be burned; as a result he cannot envisage his end without trembling. The Apostle may have wished to depart and be with Christ; 'for myself,' says Origen the preacher, 'I cannot speak thus,' and he gives to these words, by his use of the first person, the quality of a personal confession.[12] Of course he knows that this sense of sin is not shared by most men, but because he holds it necessary for a truly Christian life, he intends to lead his hearers to it by turning their attention to the universally sinful condition of men.

The sinner must humble himself; he must bring forth 'fruits of repentance'; when thinking of the judgement to come, he must address God with prayers accompanied by intense weeping; he must hold himself inwardly ready to take willingly upon himself any hardship that God sends him; he must know how to wait patiently for the mercy of God. Examining all this in detail, one finds marked ascetic tendencies throughout . . . . Already noticeable in the earliest writings of the second century, they now emerge more sharply, making Origen appear once again as a precursor of monasticism.

The spiritual man will remember that with the growth of perfection temptations also become stronger; he will therefore have to live in a perpetual awareness of sin.[13]

This 'awareness of sin' is nothing other than perpetual compunction. The word itself in fact is used by Origen. Saint Paul, the prototype of the spiritual man, *multum compunctus est, non semel, sed semper.*[14] These excellent

observations of a scholar who has so profoundly penetrated
into the spirit of Origen show that simpler men had someone
to refer to when they preached or put these teachings into
practice.

After Origen came a swarm of quite orthodox writers
endlessly preaching the necessity and usefulness of *penthos.*
Among them are the most famous fathers of the Church:
Saint Athanasius, Saint Basil in his *Rules* and elsewhere,
Saint Gregory Nazianzen in various homilies, Saint Gregory
of Nyssa in the *Beatitudes,* Saint John Chrysostom in a
special treatise on the subject, and Saint Ephrem who in his
Syriac and Greek works returns to it over and over again.
Then there is the basic charter of monasticism, the *Apophthegmata of the Fathers* or the *Verba Seniorum.* In the latter
there is a *libellus* (III) *De compunctione.* There are such
great spiritual writers as Evagrius; Cassian, a witness to
Eastern spirituality whose work is at least partially translated
into Greek; Saint Nilus, who tells us in a letter that he has
written a treatise on compunction;[15] Abba Isaiah; Antiochus
who devotes the entire ninetieth homily of his *Pandect* to the
topic; Saint John Climacus, entitling the seventh degree of
his *Ladder* Περὶ τοῦ χαροποιοῦ πένθους; Saint Barsanuphius
and John the Prophet in their letters of direction. Mark the
Hermit, although he never uses the word *penthos,* must
nevertheless be mentioned here as having undertaken to
prove against the Messalians that repentance is necessary for
everyone up to the moment of death. So the tradition continues through the centuries with men like Simeon Studite,
his disciple Symeon the New Theologian and his disciple
Nicetas Stethatos, Peter of Damascus, Theoleptus of Phila-
delphia, Neophyte the Recluse, the two Xanthopoulos, and
others. The subject became such a literary commonplace that
the Emperor Leo VI felt something would be lacking from
his glory if he did not try his hand at it like everyone else.[16]
Manuel Paleologus put 'catanyctic chapters' into verse,[17]
and 'catanyctic iambics' may be seen in PG 117:1189-1194.

Then, when people were no longer familiar with the *Katharevousa,* books in common Greek insured the continuation of the doctrine, as the seventeenth-century work of Marinos Tsanes Bouniales, entitled Κατάνυξις ὠφέλιμος διὰ κάθε χριστιανόν.[18] The champion of spiritual renewal at the end of the eighteenth century, Nicodemus the Hagiorite, would never have permitted himself so to abuse the tradition as not to have published a volume of 'catanyctic' prayers, including a preface which is in fact a complete treatise.[19] There are still others to be mentioned.

This religious tendency is equally evident in translations of foreign authors. Why was Saint Gregory the Great, surnamed Dialogos, so quickly put into Greek, and why did he enjoy such popularity? Might it not be because he was the Latins' great doctor of compunction?[20] Cassian has already been mentioned. As soon as they made the acquaintance of Saint Augustine, the Eastern ascetics preferred above all his ability to awaken the feeling of compunction. The very title *Kekragarion,* given to the first printed collection of his works, adequately reveals the preoccupation which guided this choice.[21] Among the Syrians, Saint Ephrem was translated into Greek in his lifetime; we already know how untiring he was on the topic. Isaac of Nineveh, so different from Ephrem on the other points, resembled him in this. He, too, was not long in receiving the honor of a Greek translation.

As for the Syrians who were not translated, we mention here only James of Sarug and John the Solitary (the false John of Lycopolis), whose ideas on tears merit special notice. The doctrine of *penthos* was so deeply ingrained in the Syriac-speaking Christians that the very word of the second beatitude (πενθοῦντες = 'abîlā) became the name for monks. Among the Armenians, the most famous book in their literature, the *Narek,* or the ninety-two *Sacred Elegies* of Gregory of Narek, might well be entitled *Kekragarion* or 'catanyctic prayers'. Then there is Narses Chenorhali and, in the twelfth century, Gregory the Philosopher, who wrote a

*Book of Laments.* We will of course make here the greatest use of Greek works, since it was Byzantium which dominated all of Eastern spirituality. And if we had to illustrate the doctrine with some examples, what a cloud of witnesses we would have in the *Lives* of the saints!

# IV

## DEFINING *PENTHOS*

TO GIVE SOME ORDER to the teachings scattered throughout this multitude of documents, we will attempt first to give a definition of *penthos,* after which we will consider its causes and effects: first the cause in its strictest sense; then the means used to apply this cause subjectively (this is the literal meaning of κατάνυξις); finally what disposes the subject to receive this stimulus, that is, favorable circumstances. These will be better understood by contrast with unfavorable circumstances which harm compunction or cause it to disappear altogether. The effects will be divided into those which are invisible and those which are psychological.

While definitions of *penthos* are not lacking, none of them is quite satisfactory. The spiritual masters cared little for proximate type and specific difference. Nicetas Stethatos, with just a hint of pedantry, devoted part of his *Centuries* to making precise certain points concerning ascetic vocabulary. All he gained from this was to separate himself further from the tradition. For him compunction (κατάνυξις) had ceased to be what it had been for all the ancients since Saint John Chrysostom, and now became exclusively a higher charism.[1] This is an undue restriction of the word's meaning. Saint John Climacus used his accustomed method: an accumulation of ὅροι, each of which presents a new aspect of virtue or vice to be described. At the end the reader may, if he has a scholastic temperament, construct for himself a proper definition. From the twelfth century comes this one,

17

taken from the *Life* of Saint Cyril of Philea by Nicholas Kataskepenos: '*Penthos* is godly sorrow, engendered by repentance; *penthos* is a feeling accompanied by sadness and suffering because of the privation of what gives joy.'[2] Perhaps this could be shortened. Saint Gregory of Nyssa writes, '*Penthos* (in general) is a sorrowful disposition of the soul, caused by the privation of something desirable'.[3]

From a christian point of view there is one word which expresses all that is desirable: salvation. Nothing but what endangers salvation, then, should make us sad. Here is the place to reread, but now in full, the saying of Saint Barsanuphius given on page 4: 'One must absolutely not be saddened by anything in this world, but only by sin'. Saint John Chrysostom had already taught that, in beings destined for eternity, the only justifiable sorrow is for the loss of eternal happiness through sin. Here then is the first concept of *penthos: mourning for lost salvation,* whether one's own or that of others.

A word of explanation is needed concerning these two terms: mourning and salvation. One must be careful not to confuse compunction with penance. Compunction goes much further; first of all, further back in time. No-one ever had a higher or more daring concept of the divine goodness than those specialists in *penthos,* the desert fathers.

> A brother questioned Abba Poemen saying, 'I have committed a great sin and I want to do penance for three years.' The old man said to him, 'That is a lot.' The brother said, 'For one year?' The old man said again, 'That is a lot.' Those who were present said, 'For forty days?' He said again, 'That is a lot.' He added, 'I myself say that if a man repents with his whole heart and does not intend to commit the sin any more, God will accept him after only three days.'

Better still:

> A brother said to Abba Poemen, 'If I fall into a

shameful sin, my conscience devours and accuses
me saying: "Why have you fallen?" ' The old man
said to him, 'At the moment when a man goes
astray, if he says, I have sinned, immediately the
sin ceases.'[4]
The same Poemen can be heard singing the praises of *penthos*
in all keys, endlessly declaring its necessity.
   Abba Moses is no less an optimist:

> A brother asked the old man, 'Here is a man who
> beats his servant because of a fault he has com-
> mitted; what will the servant say?' The old man
> said, 'If the servant is good, he should say, "For-
> give me, I have sinned".' The brother said to him,
> 'Nothing else?' The old man said, 'No, for from the
> moment he takes upon himself the responsibility
> for the affair and says, "I have sinned," immediately
> his master will have mercy on him.'[5]

Yet Moses would have us always conscious that we are sinners.[6] Abba Sisoes repeats almost word for word the saying
of Poemen on the rapid effect of repentance; but he says
elsewhere, 'I go to sleep in [the remembrance of] sin and
I awaken in [the remembrance of] sin.'[7]
   No ancient spiritual writer is more earnest in urging
meditation on divine goodness than Mark the Hermit, the
preacher of perpetual repentance.[8] One wonders if he had
not reversed the traditional order of virtues when he recommended that his Nicholas begin with the perpetual remembrance of God's benefits.[9] All he was really asking was that
'godly sorrow' go together with thanksgiving: εὐχαριστία
μετὰ συντετριμμένης ψυχῆς.[10] You cannot have one without
the other. *Penthos*[11] without thanksgiving would be despair,
sorrow that was not godly, while thanksgiving without
repentance would be a presumptuous illusion. Two further
points show that Mark does not use the term μετάνοια in its
strict sense. First, while penance is clearly personal, so that
one cannot offer it for the sins of others, nevertheless one

can feel grief for them. 'Saints should offer repentance to God for their neighbor, for they cannot achieve perfection without charity in deed.'[12] Secondly, penance in its strict sense must be concerned with specific sins. Once past faults have been forgiven, it is not proper to recall them one by one. 'This detailed recollection is harmful to hope if it is accompanied with sadness; if it is done without sadness, it will lead you back to your previous filth.'[13] In a word, penance in the strict sense has an end; that which has no end is what common ascetic usage calls compunction.[14]

The necessity for *penthos* after the remission of sins is upheld by Origen's doctrine of the traces of sin in the soul. Fifteen centuries after the Alexandrian master, Nicodemus the Hagiorite repeated his teaching, relying on unimpeachable authorities.

> The second reason why repentance must be perpetual is that each sin is like a wound. However well the wound may heal, the scar, the mark, the imprint ($\tau\acute{\upsilon}\pi o\varsigma$) of the sin remains in the soul; it is impossible to efface it completely, as most, if not all, theologians agree. He who has stolen once, or fornicated, or murdered, can never again become as innocent and pure as if he had never stolen or fornicated or murdered. That is why, each time the sinner thinks back on the sins he has committed and observes the imprints and marks of his wound, he cannot but be saddened, weep, and repent, even if we assume that his wounds have been healed. The scars and marks of all sins thus remain ineffaceably in the soul, as we have said, but more especially those of sins of the flesh. The great Basil in his discourse on virginity says that repentance can remit the sin of a man or woman, but it cannot for all that cause a woman who has lost her virginity to be as if she had never lost it and had remained a virgin.

This fact of itself brings *penthos* for the rest of their lives to those who have fornicated.

Repentance can remit sins, but it cannot restore virginity to a woman who has lost it. She must lament this loss for the rest of her life. How can what was spoiled become unspoiled? How can what has once been violated by desire, corruption and passion become inviolate, when signs of corruption remain in the body and the soul?'[15]

Toward the end of his discourse on repentance, Mark says: There can be healing even after an ulcer, but the scar remains. Saint Gregory says, 'There is no restoration to our previous condition, even if we should seek it with many sighs and tears. From the latter comes the scar tissue, painfully to be sure, but we may be sure that it comes. As for removing the scars, I wish it were possible, for I too have need of forgiveness.' (*Sermon on Baptism*). Cyril of Jerusalem says this: 'The stains of sins remain in the body even as a wound which, although treated, leaves a scar. Sin wounds both body and soul, and the imprints of its nails remain in everyone.' Isidore of Pelusium is of the same opinion when he says, 'Now that you have heard that repentance is possible, do not begin to sin without fear, under the pretext that you will certainly find healing. You must know, first, that many have not even had the time to repent. When they were still gone astray, they were called to render their accounts. Again, repentance usually requires considerable time for curing the passions. Labors, fasting, vigils, alms, prayers and all other remedies of this sort are necessary to heal previous wounds. In the third place, we must be on our guard since, even after healing, the scar reveals the disease. An uninjured body is not the same as one that is cured, any more than untorn clothing resembles what has been torn,

even when skillful work has restored it to such a
condition that it is difficult to find any fault with
it.' (*Letter 157* to Casios). Healing is the closing of
a wound, concerning which God speaks through
Jeremiah, 'They have healed the wound of my
people lightly' (Jer 6:14). And the great Athanasius says, 'He who repents ceases to sin, but he
keeps the scars from his wounds'. Saint Chrysostom does, to be sure, say that 'God, when he
erases sins, does not leave a scar, does not even
allow a trace to remain, but with health he restores
even beauty.' (Discourses on repentance, beginning
with the words, 'Although yesterday I was deprived
of you.') This, however, is said concerning God's
infinite love of man, not repentance, which cannot
of itself do this. The same Chrysostom continues
at this place, explaining what he has said: 'Not that
repentance can of itself wipe out sin, but because
repentance combines with God's ineffable love for
man and his infinite goodness . . . ' .

Although not compelled to it in his polemic against the
Messalians, Mark the Hermit might have done better to
distinguish repentance from *penthos,* as John Climacus
would later do, discussing each one in a separate chapter.[16]
The *Verba Seniorum* speak of compunction in one place and
of repentance in another.[17] The point is aptly illustrated in
the latter text by the title of chapter 23: *That through
repentance man may some day be reconciled with God—
Quod per poenitentiam uno die potest homo reconciliari
Deo.*[18]

Theophanes Cerameus, archbishop of Taormina in the
twelfth century, sees two dispositions of the soul expressed
in the wording of the second beatitude:

The *penthos* worthy of being blessed is that which
mourns for transgressions and sins. Through it we
obtain the consolation of divine pity. But the

durative sense of the verb makes us understand yet
another *penthos.* Christ did not say, 'Blessed are
those who have wept,' but 'those who weep,' that
is, who constantly remember the glory from which
they have fallen and how they have been lament-
ably exiled in this place of tears. They make their
mourning unceasing and obtain consolation.[19]

Psychologically, *penthos* goes still further. Its very name,
its two names, are words of sentiment. A cold and merely
willed repentance would not do, even if, from a theologian's
point of view, it were worth more than any felt emotion.
Tears may not be necessary for true contrition, but *penthos*
cannot exist without them. So essential was this aspect of
feeling that it would end by taking precedence over the
consideration of lost salvation, although without ever obli-
terating it. Compunction was to become the name for all
emotions which come from supernatural thought. The rough
stalk of *penthos*-mourning was to be covered with so many
flowers springing from its sap that the bitter root would
almost be forgotten; yet it is always there, and necessary to
the plant. 'Godly sorrow' and its equivalents would be the
highest expression of joy here below: Χαροποιὸν πένθος. The
evangelical beatitude was to be realized in this world:
'Blessed are the πενθοῦντες, for they will be comforted'.
'Mourning' would now be the equivalent of consolation, even
more, of happiness.

'Salvation' is not just a matter of avoiding hell and some-
how getting into heaven. It is, as its etymology indicates, the
wholeness of good health. Present-day Italian still says
*la salute,* with the two meanings of health and salvation.
No-one is healthy who has any sort of infirmity. Every fault,
even the smallest and least noticeable, means the contamina-
tion of a little health, a little 'salvation'. Integral salvation
would suppose that at no moment of his life would a man
have failed to acquire the degree of perfection possible to
him. Who could make this boast? Abba Isaiah said, 'Even if a

man should have the power to work miracles and cures, and if he should possess all knowledge and could raise the dead, if he once falls into sin he cannot be carefree, because he is subject to repentance.'[20] Going further, Mark the Hermit did not hesitate to say that if one should in fact have attained to perfection, it would still be true that he *has been* a sinner, if only by virtue of original sin.[21] Baptismal innocence, no matter how jealously guarded, will not take away from anyone the status of being 'redeemed by Christ', and it is to all the redeemed, without exception, that the Redeemer says, 'Repent'. If repentance is necessary, so *a fortiori* is 'sorrow'. Monks, called πενθικοί in Syria, earn this name precisely because their profession is to be οἱ σώζεσθαι βουλόμενοι, those who mean to work out their salvation. Whereas the constitutions of more modern orders propose to their members the goals of 'salvation and perfection', Saint Basil thought he had said it all when he wrote, 'The ascetic life has a single goal, the salvation of the soul'.[22] The monk, at least the eastern monk, is not a special person. He merely claims to be taking Christianity seriously.

It is because salvation is rarely, if ever, in its proper state, and certainly never perfected in this life, that we shall learn from all sides of the necessity of compunction, a necessity which never ends. To him who has arrived at *apatheia,* and who therefore has no further need of purification or mortification, Evagrius recommends, 'Remember your previous life and your former faults, and how, although full of passions, you have through Christ's mercy attained to a passionless state'.[23] It will come as no surprise that the same author—an intellectual and a philosopher—should have preached the necessity of tears at all three stages of the spiritual life: 'First pray for the gift of tears, to soften by compunction the inherent hardness of your soul, and then, as you confess your sinfulness to the Lord, to obtain pardon from him'. Even when this pardon is obtained, tears are still needed 'to obtain all our requests',[24] it being understood that all our

requests should concern nothing but salvation. There will be
a time when 'the perfect man will no longer practice mortification,'[25] but it will always be an illusion to imagine that
we have no further need of tears. 'If it seems to you that you
no longer need to weep in prayer for your sins, consider how
far you have gone from God ['by this thought', the Arabic
version accurately adds].[26] You should in fact be in him
unceasingly, and then you will weep the more fervently.'
The teaching of the 'Fathers' is the same: 'Going into Egypt
one day, Abba Poemen saw a woman who was sitting in a
tomb and weeping bitterly. He said, "If all the delights of the
world were to come, they could not drive sorrow away from
the soul of this woman. Even so the monk should have
compunction in himself." '[27] Abba Euprepios counts *penthos*
among the four virtues which are perpetually required.[28] We
must take it with us everywhere, like our shadow.[29] Laughter
thus becomes incomprehensible. 'An old man saw someone
laugh, and said to him, "It is before the Lord of heaven and
earth that we must render an account of our life, and you
laugh!" '[30] The most illustrious doctors of the Church share
the view of the Egyptian hermits. Saint John Chrysostom is
at one here with Saint Ephrem, as the texts will show. For
the moment it is enough to understand the nature of
*penthos.* It is mourning for salvation lost, a mourning which
must be perpetual, just as we must perpetually work out
our salvation.

V

# THE CAUSES OF COMPUNCTION

## LOSS OF SALVATION

THE CAUSE OF *PENTHOS* may be found in the definition just given, but it takes different forms, and works in various ways. To these we now turn. First there is salvation, in the technical sense, to which is opposed mortal sin. Here are some texts, taken at random from the mass of those which come to mind.

As in the natural order we weep for the dead [writes Saint John Chrysostom], so should we weep—to put it no more strongly—for our salvation. It is with such desire and courage that we all should keep the eye of our soul trained to this end; everything should serve us as a reminder of it. Those who have lost their children or their wives can think of nothing but their lost ones, whereas we who have lost a heavenly kingdom think of anything rather than that. No bereaved man, even of the most royal stock, will be ashamed to submit to the law of mourning. He will throw himself on the ground, will weep bitterly, will change his clothing, will gladly undergo all the other manifestations which are fitting at such a time, and this without any thought of his training, or of the infirmities that might follow such affliction. He will undergo all this without the slightest difficulty . . . . And we who are in mourning not for a wife or

26

child but for a soul and not for another's soul but for our own, we excuse ourselves on the pretext of delicate health or an advanced education! And if only this were the worst of it! But we neglect even what requires no physical effort. What bodily strength is needed, I ask you, for contriteness of heart, for vigilant prayer, for reflection on our sins, for beating back the growth of foolish presumption, for humbling the understanding? That is what would make God favorable to us, but we do not even do that much.[1]

As for Saint Ephrem, we would have to cite almost everything he wrote. The author of his eulogy, attributed to Saint Gregory of Nyssa, writes,

When I start to remember his floods of tears I myself begin to weep, for it is almost impossible to pass dry-eyed through the ocean of his tears. There was never a day or night, or part of a day or night, or any moment, however short, when his vigilant eyes did not appear bathed in tears. Sometimes, as he said, it was the misery and folly common to all that he wept for, sometimes particular vices. Nor was it just when he spoke of penance, morals, or the ruling of life that you would find him weeping and moaning, but even in prayer of praise.[2]

It should be noted in passing that although many of the printed or manuscript works attributed to Ephrem are probably not authentic, they are for all that documents of Eastern spirituality. They have been read with the respect due to their true or supposed author by innumerable faithful in all the countries of the East. Here is just an example:

The soul is dead through sin. It requires sadness, weeping, tears, mourning and bitter moaning over the iniquity which has cast it down to perdition. Howl, weep and moan, and bring it back to God.

See how the mother suffers whose child has been
snatched away by death and thrown in the tomb;
she laments because her love has departed. Even
greater sadness should be in a man whom sin has
separated from God, that such a lovely image of his
goodness should be lost. If you own an animal and
it dies, you feel the loss. Even if you have just
recently acquired it, you bear the grief of its death.
God is distressed because of the image which has
been lost to him. A soul is far dearer to him than
the rest of his creation. Through sin it becomes
dead, and you, sinner, think nothing of this! You
should rather grieve for the sake of this God who
grieves for you. Your soul is dead through vice;
shed tears and raise it up again! Give God this joy,
to rejoice that you have raised up your soul
again . . . . Weep and moan for your soul,
separated from God, this God who is distressed for
you as a mother for her only child. One who laughs
near a corpse must hate the dead person's parents.
If on the other hand one is sorrowful, he shows his
love in weeping. So it is that one who rejoices while
he is dead through sin must hate God, who experiences suffering and sorrow. God is in mourning
and sadness for the dead soul, and one who laughs
and makes light of this thereby increases God's
suffering, as one who acts this way increases the
suffering and sadness of one whose child is being
buried. A man falls into sin and rejoices; this causes
even further grief in God. A father who has buried
a beloved child feels nothing like the grief which
God feels for a soul killed by iniquity. Put on
mourning, then, for your soul, and show your love
for God, who experiences suffering and sorrow for
the sinful and dead soul. God is grieved for the soul
which is his image. One who rejoices and does not

suffer exactly resembles Satan. One who comes
near a dead person sees the mourning going on for
him; his spirit is overcome with suffering and he
shares the mourners' sorrow. A soul has died from
iniquity, and the lament rises to heaven; the celes-
tial armies are grieved, and God himself is greatly
troubled. One who loves joy and refuses to weep
over his soul is in truth a reprobate who knows
not that he has a soul. Weep over your soul, sinner,
shed tears and raise it up again. Its resurrection
depends on your eyes, and its return to life on your
heart. You are dead, and you do not weep at being
separated from your soul! Weep over yourself first,
and then you will weep for others. Over a dead
body you weep, but over a soul dead and separated
from God you do not weep! Tears falling on a
corpse cannot restore it, but if they fall on a soul
they will bring it back to life. It is not for the
body that tears, sorrow, and affliction were made.
It is for the soul that God made them, so that you
may raise it up again. Give God weeping, and increase the tears in your eyes: through your tears
and his goodness the soul which had been dead will
be restored. Behold, Mercy waits for your eyes to
shed tears, to purify and renew the image of the
disfigured soul. It is you who have put to death
your soul, and it is you who must raise it up
again from iniquity. It is not another which has
killed and destroyed you; you have done this to
yourself through your own will. If another had
done this, it is he who would have to raise you up,
but since it is your will which has brought death
to you, it is your will which must bring you back
to life.[3]

While it might be suggested that these two Syrians,
Chrysostom and Ephrem, have perhaps done no more here

than give way to their natural harshness of temperament, this is one suspicion to which Saint Gregory Nazianzen could never be subject. He might rather be accused of excessive timidity. He alone is called 'the theologian', chiefly because of his constant concern with man's deification, and for this reason he deserves an attentive hearing. Here Gregory is writing about a natural calamity, but he reasons about it exactly as did Ephrem, only in another style:

You too, imitate the timid priest [himself]. Yes, my beloved children, yes, you who have a share with him in the divine admonition and goodness, keep your souls in tears. Forestall his anger by improving your actions . . . . I know that this holds for me, a minister of the Lord, and for you who have received the same honor: we must enter [into the sanctuary] clothed in sackcloth and must beat our breast night and day between the threshold and the altar. In pitiable dress and in a still more pitiable voice, let us cry out earnestly for ourselves and for the people, sparing neither effort nor words which might bend God to us . . . . We should afflict ourselves all the more since our dignity is greater, and so by our example teach the people compunction (*catanyxis*) and the correction of evil . . . . Come then, brothers, let us all prostrate ourselves and weep before the Lord our creator. Let us organize a common mourning (*penthos*), dividing ourselves according to age and station. Let us raise the voice of supplication. Instead of cries which are hateful to him, let us rather send up this cry to the Lord of hosts: 'Let us forestall his anger with confession'. Now that we have seen him provoked, let us undertake to bring him back from his anger. Who knows, it has been written, if he will not repent and leave us a blessing. How well I know, I who have benefited

from the divine love for man. He will forsake what
is contrary to his nature, wrath, for what is con-
formable to it, mercy. It is, after all, to this end
that he does us violence; this is the way he always
leans . . . . Only let us take pity on ourselves, and
beat a path to the righteous tenderness of the
father. Let us sow in tears, to reap in joy.[4]

As for the tears of monks, we know what Saint Gregory
thought of them: 'They are the deluge [falling on] sins, the
purification of the world.'[5] One feels that he longed for
these tears, just as he so desired solitude. After all, did he not
expressly ask for them?[6] The ninety-nine *Poems on himself*
are scarcely anything but a succession of *threni*. To take only
one line, which goes to the heart of the matter:

Δάκρυε, δακρυ' ἀλιτρέ · τὸ σὸν μόνον ἐστὶν ὄνειαρ.

*Weep, sinner, weep; you have no recourse but this.*[7]

It would be too easy to keep multiplying examples. In the
case of grave sins which must be expiated, compunction
becomes something very close to penance, in the strict sense
of the word, but draws into it an element of sensitivity which,
at least to us moderns, does not seem essential to the sacrament. Perhaps our ancestors thought otherwise. This is not
the place to raise questions belonging to the historical tract
*de poenitentia.* It can, however, be safely said that the sacrament of penance was once practised less frequently than
today. Thus, an author such as Saint Ephrem will speak little
of the sacrament but much of the *virtue* of repentance. The
multiplication of confessions has had its part to play in the
gradual dying out of compunction.

On the other hand, as we saw in our discussions of sources,
the traditional doctrine has been well guarded in the East. To
this any orthodox catechism will bear witness, with its
division according to the three theological virtues, of which
the second, on hope, follows the Beatitudes. Here is
Peter Moghila:

What does the second beatitude teach? This beatitude teaches that among the orthodox those are happy who at all times of their life are sorry and weep for the sins by which they have offended God and their neighbor, according to the prophet: 'The children of Israel shall come, they and the people of Judah. They shall go weeping, and they shall seek the Lord their God' (Jer 50:4). Those do not share in this beatitude who weep for some worldly passion.[8]

Intensity of tears must correspond to gravity of faults. Two brothers according to the flesh renounced the world and went to live under obedience to a father in the mountain of Nitria. God gave to both of them the gift of tears and compunction. One day, in a vision, the old man saw the two brothers in prayer, each holding in his hand a written parchment and bathing it with his tears. Now the writing on one of them was easily effaced, but that on the other with difficulty; it seemed to be written with indelible ink. The old man asked for an explanation of the vision, and an angel of the Lord came to tell him this: 'On these parchments are the sins of each man. But one sinned according to nature, and so his faults are easily wiped out, whereas the other has soiled himself with impurities and hideous crimes against nature. Hence, he needs greater efforts to repent fittingly and to humble himself deeply.' From that time, the old man would say to this brother, 'Exert yourself, brother, because indelible ink is hard to remove.' He never revealed the vision to him until his death, so as not to discourage him. He simply kept repeating to him, 'Exert yourself, because it's indelible'.[9]

As for the brother who had sinned less, the good old man said nothing to him at all. It might then happen that the less guilty would think himself the greater sinner. This is an ordinary occurence in the lives of saints, and of others as well. Ancient hagiography seems to have been less concerned than later literature to proclaim that its heroes had maintained baptismal innocence. As for the heroes themselves, they were in their own eyes the most wretched of men: *peccatores . . . quorum primus ego.* They would have thought it unforgivably arrogant to hold that the teaching of the doctors on compunction was exaggerated, or that they themselves were exceptions to the common law. Instead, we see them striving to equal the great models, Saint Ephrem for the Syrians or Saint Arsenius for the Greeks; above all, Saint Arsenius—the most elegant courtier of the imperial palace become the most squalidly clad of the solitaries, the great man of letters, roman or hellenic, longing for 'the alphabet of the Egyptian peasants,'[10] that is, their practical science of the spiritual life. 'It was said of Abba Arsenius that throughout his life, whenever he sat at manual labor, he tucked a handkerchief under his chin because of the tears that flowed from his eyes.'[11] Nor were these merely tears of consolation:

> When his death drew near, the brethren saw him weeping and they said to him, 'Truly, Father, are you also afraid?' 'Indeed,' he answered them, 'the fear which is on me at this hour has been with me ever since I became a monk.' Upon this he fell asleep.[12]

The most fervent ascetics dreamed constantly of becoming 'another great Arsenius'.[13] It would be an interesting subject for an historian of spirituality to trace through the ages the influence of a saint on the particular cast of christian life in a given country. For Arsenius, one would have to examine the entire East.

## THE CERTAINTY OF DEATH AND JUDGEMENT

It is then in remembrance of past sins that compunction finds its chief stimulant, but it is also sustained by the certainties and uncertainties of the future.

A brother fervent in prayer, while saying the office with his own brother, would be overcome by tears and sometimes omit a psalm verse. One day his brother begged him to say what he was thinking of during the office, to make him weep so bitterly. He said, 'Forgive me, brother, during the office I always contemplate the Judge and myself before him, a guilty criminal undergoing interrogation. Knowing no excuse for myself, I stand horrified, my mouth closes, and I let a psalm verse go by. Forgive me for annoying you. If you prefer, let us recite the office separately.' The brother replied, 'No, Father, for if I have no compunction, at least in seeing you I will be ashamed.' And God, seeing his humility, gave him also the compunction which his brother had. Let us also try to keep our eyes on those who have this gift, and we will gain the same advantage as this brother.[14]

At Raithon there was an old hesychast who had the following practice. He remained sitting in his cell, solemn and with eyes downcast, constantly shaking his head and saying with groans, 'What will happen to me?' Then he would remain silent awhile, and again say the same words with the same gestures. But at the same time he worked at his weaving, and thus he spent all his days meditating on his salvation.[15]

Possibilities of future sins: in his *Synagogē,* Paul Evergetinus has a long chapter on this uncertainty of final victory:

> One old man met another, and as they conversed
> one of them said, 'As for me, I am dead to the
> world'. But the other said, 'Do not be too sure,
> brother, as long as you have not left your body. It
> is useless to say, "I am dead." Satan is not dead.'

> Satan presented himself to a holy man at the hour
> of his death and said, 'You have beaten me'. The
> old man answered, 'I still do not know.'[16]

Saint Ephrem qualified sin as εὐπερίστατος, that which besets
us easily.[17] Peter of Damascus, whose work is a catena of
patristic texts, entitled one chapter of his compilation, 'On
the second commandment: the origin of *penthos* is fear'.[18]
Saint John Chrysostom had already treated the subject with
eloquence. After listing many other happy effects of fear, he
continues, 'And these are not the only fruits which fear
produces; there is yet another of greater price . . . . There
where fear is, are also found burning and uninterrupted tears
and the groans of a deep compunction.'[19] 'A brother
questioned Abba Poemen, "What ought I to do about all the
turmoils that trouble me?" The old man said to him, "In all
our afflictions let us weep in the presence of the goodness of
God, until he shows mercy on us".'[20]


DAILY FAULTS

There are not only grave sins, but the daily faults of the just
man who falls seven times a day. They too draw tears from
'those who wish to be saved'. Scepticism has sometimes
been expressed about the tenderness of the desert fathers'
conscience.[21] Nothing discredits such doubts more than the
seriousness with which these holy men considered the little
failings caused by human weakness. Before judging these
men, we should learn their language and their philosophy.

'The beginning of salvation,' goes a pithy saying of Saint Nilus, 'is to condemn oneself.'[22] It is the beginning, yes, and still more the end. 'Abba Matoes said, "The nearer a man draws to God, the more he sees himself a sinner. It was when Isaiah the prophet saw God, that he declared himself a man of unclean lips".'[23] The chapter of Evergetinos from which this apophthegm is drawn, one of the longest of the *Synagogē*, has as its title, 'That it befits a humble man to blame and disparage himself, and to count as nothing the works he performs, whatever may be their quantity and quality'. The next chapter continues the same subject, adding that one must judge no-one but rather, in any adversity, attribute the fault to oneself alone. Whoever wishes to practise this rule will not lack for opportunities to 'blame himself', and thus find many motives for compunction. Such a one was Saint Dosithy:

> This young man was very gentle in all his work. He served the sick in the hospital, and all were comforted by his services. He did everything with care. If, however, he happened to be negligent with one of the patients, or even to speak an ill-tempered word to him, then he would drop everything and go in tears to the storeroom. The hospital attendants would come to console him, but it was no use. They would then go and say to Abba Dorotheos, 'Master, please go and see what is the matter with this brother. He is weeping, and we do not know why.' And so he would go and find him seated on the ground, still weeping. He would say, 'What is it, Dosithy? What is the matter with you? Why are you weeping?' And he would reply, 'Forgive me, Master, I was angry and I spoke harshly to my brother.' Then Dorotheos would say, 'Yes, Dosithy, you do get angry! And you are not ashamed of being angry and of speaking harshly to your brother . . . . Do you not know

that he is Christ, and that it is Christ whom you
are making sad?' And he would lower his eyes,
weeping in silence. When, then, Dorotheos saw
that he had wept enough, he would end by saying,
'May God forgive you! Come on! Let us begin
again from this moment. Let us be more careful in
future, and may God come to our aid.' As soon
as he heard this, Dosithy would get up and run
with joy to his work, persuaded that he had
received pardon even from God. Knowing him as
they did, the hospital staff, whenever they saw him
in tears, would say, 'Now what is the matter with
Dosithy? What has he done wrong?' And they
would say to the blessed Dorotheos, 'Master, you
had better go to the storeroom; there is work for
you there.' And so he would go and find Dosithy
seated on the ground in tears. He would know
that he had said something disagreeable, and would
say to him, 'What is the matter, Dosithy? Have
you saddened Christ again? Become angry again?
Are you not ashamed? Will you never learn?' And
he would continue to weep. Again, when he saw
him sated with weeping, Dorotheos would say to
him, 'Come on! May God pardon you! Once more,
start all over again. Correct yourself from now
on.' And he, at that moment, would confidently
shake off his sadness and go to his work.[24]

Dosithy was a child, but we will see that compunction is
hardly an aspect of youth. The author of the *Life* admitted
that his purpose was chiefly to give a model of childlike
obedience. Others would not think themselves pardoned so
easily, and it is not without reason that we so often hear
their spiritual fathers warning them against discouragement.
*Penthos* was always in danger of giving way to sadness, its
dangerous counterfeit. It required heroism to condemn oneself constantly without ever resigning oneself to what one

condemned. And then the very occupations of the ascetic, his concentration on God, the examples of others, the exhortations he received, all conspired to increase in him a horror of the slightest failings. He would find in the liturgy, taking this as seriously as he did, something more than mere occasions for ecstasy.

A brother met one of the elders in the laura of Soucas above Jericho and said to him, 'How is it with you, Father?' The old man replied, 'Badly!' The brother asked, 'Why, Father?' The old man said, 'Here have I been for thirty years, standing before God in prayer, and I condemn myself every time I say to God, "Spare none of those who treacherously plot evil", and again, "Cursed are those who depart from your commandments", for I depart from them every day and commit iniquity. Yet again I say to God, "You destroy those who speak lies", and I lie every day. While I harbor perverse thoughts in my heart I tell God, "The meditations of my heart is always before you". I, who certainly do not fast, say, "My knees are weak through fasting". And again, I bear a grudge against my brother, and I say to God, "Forgive us as we forgive". Even though I think of nothing but eating my bread, I say, "I forget to eat my bread". I who sleep until morning still chant the words, "At midnight I rise to praise you". Having no compunction, I say, "I grow weary with crying, and tears have become my food day and night". Full of pride and fleshly comfort, I make a fool of myself by saying, "See my humility and sorrow, and forgive me all my sins". I am not at all ready, and I say, "My heart is ready, O God". In a word, the whole liturgy and my prayer have turned into a reproach and a dishonor for me.' The brother said, 'I think, Father, that David said all that in speaking of himself.' But the old man replied, moaning, 'What are you saying, brother? Certainly, if we do not observe what we sing before God, we will go to perdition.'[25]

No doubt this holy man is judging himself harshly, at least by our standards. Whatever an insensitive conscience may be, this is not it. At one point though his confession contradicts itself—when he accuses himself of having no compunction at all. His 'groans' give the lie to this excess of zeal in 'blaming himself'. His interlocutor certainly was not fooled, if we may believe another passage where the beginning of the same story is repeated, but with this conclusion, 'And the brother was greatly edified by the old man's humility'.[26] What would he have said of Saint Macarius?

> Abba Paphnutius, the disciple of Abba Macarius, repeated this saying of the old man, 'When I was little, with other children I used to eat bilberries and they used to go and steal little figs. As they were running away, they dropped one of the figs, and I picked it up and ate it. Every time I remember this, I sit down and weep.[27]

Saint Theodore of Tabennisi once had an ambitious thought, and he admitted it to Saint Pachomius. Everyone held that this was no sin, but Pachomius thought otherwise. He spoke to his presumptive heir in such sharp terms that 'Theodore arose in great distress. He withdrew into a cell at some distance to give himself up to *penthos* with intense tears and sadness, fearing that God might have turned his face from him.' This mourning lasted two years, and it was in fact Petronius whom Pachomius chose as his successor.[28]

Concerning harshness in judging oneself, it is important to remember the Stoic principle of the oneness of virtue.[29] This was very much in vogue with Christians. 'Let the true Gnostic strive to practise all virtues equally, so that they may be linked together,[30] not only in themselves but also in him, for the intellect is usually betrayed by whichever

one is lacking.'[31]  A Greek *sermo asceticus* published under
the name of Saint Ephrem seems to comment on this saying,
drawing from it a point about compunction:

> Strive to acquire perfect virtue, adorned with all
> that is pleasing to God. This is called the one
> virtue which includes in itself the beauty and
> variety of all the virtues. As a royal crown cannot
> be made without the best selection of jewels and
> pearls, so the single (μονοειδής) virtue cannot sub-
> sist without the beauty of various virtues. In fact,
> the resemblance to a royal crown is perfect: just
> as, if a stone or pearl is missing, the crown cannot
> shine on the king's head, so, if this virtue is lacking
> the lustre of one of the other virtues, it does not
> deserve the name of perfect virtue . . . . [32] Again,
> it resembles an eagle  flying aloft who, seeing his
> prey in a trap, dives at it headlong, but in seizing
> his victim he catches the end of his claw in the
> trap, and this trifling accident paralyses his whole
> strength. His body appears to be entirely free, out
> of the trap, but all his power is in fact shackled.
> So the virtue I am speaking of, whenever it
> becomes attached to an earthly object, dies from
> it, loses its strength, disappears. It can no longer go
> aloft, attached as it is to something on earth.
> Seeing this, who would not weep? If a man finds
> compunction difficult, let him observe this and
> lament: that virtue which was ascending to heaven
> and had already arrived at the gates of the king-
> dom cannot now enter.[33]

Another defect of health is stunted growth. Who then has
such unceasing care for his spiritual progress that he does
everything possible, or indeed everything desirable? Christian
perfection is so high and  our weakness so persistent, so
obstinate our power of self-deception. To advance in virtues,
as well as to escape sins, compunction is still needed. 'A

brother asked Saint Anthony, "What should I do about my sins?" The saint replied, "Whoever seeks deliverance from sins will find it in tears and weeping, and whoever wishes to advance in building up virtue will do so through weeping and tears".[34] As examples, he went on to cite King Hezekiah, Saint Peter, and Mary Magdalen who, 'after washing the Saviour's feet with her tears, deserved to hear that she had chosen the better part'. In the sayings of the fathers, it is to Abba Poemen that the same brother addresses his question, and the reply is the same, except that the scriptural quotations are summed up in a short sentence: 'Weeping is the way the Scriptures and our Fathers give us, when they say, "Weep!" Truly, there is no other way than this.'[35] Abba Moses proposes the same formula: 'Through tears we acquire virtues, just as through tears we obtain pardon for sins.'[36]

## BROTHERLY LOVE

Compunction has been defined as mourning for salvation that has been lost, either by oneself or by others. When Saint Basil declares that the ascetic life has only one goal, the salvation of the soul, he is excluding monks from the outward apostolate alone, and in no sense from either zeal or charity. Concern for the eternal destiny of others should cast us into mourning for those who are lost. At the question, 'Whether it is permitted to laugh?' Saint Basil does not understand how a good Christian can laugh 'especially when he sees how many there are who dishonor God by breaking the law and who are about to die in sin. For these we must mourn and weep'.[37] The expression Θανατουμένων ἐν τῇ ἀμαρτία probably does not mean 'who are dying in a state of sin', but 'whose soul is in a state of mortal sin'. Basil develops the thought at greater length in his homily on the martyr Julitta.

We must therefore weep with those who weep.
When you see your brother moaning in repentance
for his sins, weep with him. Thus, through the
wrongs of another, you will gain correction of your
own wrongdoing. Whoever pours out warm tears
over the sin of his neighbor cures himself by
lamenting for his brother. Such is the attitude of
him who says, 'Hot indignation seizes me because
of the wicked who foresake the law (Ps 118:53).'
Weep over sin, for it is the sickness of the soul,
the death of what is immortal; it calls for mourn-
ing ($\pi\acute{\epsilon}\nu\theta o\varsigma$) and inconsolable laments. Let endless
tears flow for it . . . . Such is the weeping, and such
the mourning which the Word beatifies, rather than
a tendency to any kind of sadness or readiness to
weep at any pretext.[38]

It will come as no surprise to meet Saint John Chrysostom
here:

And so let us not weep for the dead, but rather
for those who are dead in a state of sin. It is they
who are worthy of tears, these who deserve a show
of mourning ($\kappa o\pi\epsilon\tau\hat{\omega}\nu$) and tears . . . . Let us weep
for them, not just for a day or two, but throughout
our lives. Here are tears, not of unreasonable
passion, but rather of affection. Those which come
from unreasonable passion dry quickly, but when
the cause of tears is the fear of God, they last
forever.[39]

Moreover, this sort of mourning brings some comfort to its
dead.

Saint Theodore the Studite, at least in his old age,
preached the same sorrowful compassion:

We should pray and lament for the world. Why?
Because the Son of God came to save the world
and the world denies him. Tribes and nations deny
him. Even those who bear his name deny him,

some through their twisted beliefs, some through
their evil lives. What should he have done that he
has not done? Although God, he became man; he
humbled himself and became obedient to death,
even death on a cross; he has given us his body
to eat and his blood to drink; he has allowed himself to be called father, brother, leader, master,
spouse, co-heir, and so much more. And still he is
denied, and still he bears it. What can we say to
that, brothers? Let his true disciples lament the
denials of their fellow-servants. It is for this reason
that the great apostle orders us to make petitions,
prayers, intercessions and thanksgivings for all
men . . . . And in another place he says of himself,
'I am speaking the truth in Christ, I am not lying;
my conscience bears me witness in the Holy Spirit
that I have great sorrow and unceasing anguish in
my heart. For I would wish that I myself were
accursed and cut off from Christ for the sake of
my brethren, my kinsmen by race' (Rom 9:1-3).
And so we too, disciples legitimately born, should
not be concerned just with ourselves, but also
lament and pray for the whole world.[40]

One day Saint Anthony expressed his concern over a
young monk who had been working miracles:

After a while, Anthony suddenly began to weep,
to tear his hair and lament. His disciples said to
him, 'Why are you weeping, Father?' and the old
man replied, 'A great pillar of the Church has just
fallen (he meant the young monk) but go to him
and see what has happened.' So the disciples went
and found the monk sitting on a mat and weeping
for the sin he had committed. Seeing the disciples
of the old man he said, 'Tell the old man to pray
that God will give me just ten days and I hope I will
have made satisfaction.' But in the space of

five days he died.[41]

For others, as for oneself, salvation must be understood in a total sense, one which includes perfection. The ancient ascetics, however severely they refrained from judging any man in particular, had (perhaps like their modern counterparts) a marked tendency to pessimism when they considered aggregates, even monastic ones. That same Poemen who would not reprove another's sin even if he 'touched it with his hands', still could say frankly that 'Since Abba Moses and the third generation in Scetis, the brothers do not make progress any more'.[42] Macarius the Great—of whom it was said that he became 'a god upon earth, because, just as God protects the world, so Abba Macarius would cover the faults which he saw as though he did not see them; and those which he heard, as though he did not hear them'—even he gives this unreserved opinion of his brethren, seen as a whole: 'Abba Poemen asked him weeping; "Give me a word that I may be saved". But the old man replied, "What you are looking for has disappeared now from among monks".'[43] The expression 'old man' is to be taken here in its literal sense, since it is Poemen who is interrogating Macarius. Everyone, however, aspired to deserve this title through maturity of spirit, and one of the traits by which those honorary 'old men' could justify their name, even when they were only παιδαριογέρον- τες, was through eagerness to become *laudatores temporis acti.*

The father of monasticism had himself begun to miss the spiritual power of past generations.[44] John the Dwarf says of his generation, 'If they are given wings they are not of fire, but wings that are weak and without power.'[45] Even the most famous ascetics of the *Sayings* are not spared:

> The old men said of Abba Agathon to Abba Elias, in Egypt, 'He is a good abba'. The old man answered them, 'In comparison with his own generation, he is good'. They said to him, 'And what is he in comparison with the ancients?' He

gave them this answer, 'I have said to you that in comparison with his generation he is good but as to that of the ancients, in Scetis I have seen a man who, like Joshua the son of Nun, could make the sun stand still in the heavens.' At these words they were astounded and gave glory to God.

Again, Abba Elias said, 'In the days of our predecessors they took great care about these three virtues: poverty, obedience and fasting. But among monks nowadays avarice, self-confidence, and great greed have taken charge.'[46]

It is clear that this pessimism came both from humility, since each monk held himself to be still worse than his degenerate contemporaries, and from charity, since he considered the failings of others as his own.[47] Saint Pachomius, on behalf of ten brothers who were murmuring, 'gave himself up to *penthos* before the Lord for forty days'.[48] Hardly five years had gone by since the death of Pachomius, and already Saint Theodore exclaimed, 'Where are the old brothers?' 'After he spoke thus, he wept. The brothers wept so loud that they were heard a long distance from the divine office.'[49] Later still, 'when Theodore saw that many of them started changing the way of life of the brothers of old he went into mourning (ἐπένθησεν) for them'. He was seen going late at night to the tomb of Saint Pachomius to pray, 'Lord, even if we are neglectful, rouse us. And if we spurn you, instill fear in us and remind us of the eternal punishments.'[50]

PURE LOVE OF GOD

What inspired this *penthos* then was fraternal charity. As for the pure love of God, we must admit that at first sight, and in these words, it appears only rarely as a source of compunction. That is typical of this spirituality, convinced as it is that perfect charity, precisely because it is perfect, presupposes all

the other virtues. The theorists—Clement, Origen, Dionysius,
Maximus—speak much of pure charity; the ascetics much less,
through humility and fear of self-deception. They willingly
admit that they are weeping for the salvation they have
squandered away, but it is necessary to catch them off
guard if we wish to hear them say that this lost salvation
is primarily an offense against the love of God. Even here
they might regret, as vain boasting, the confidence drawn
from them unawares. One suspects that they always dreaded
confusing the love of God with the thought of the love of
God. Suspicious of words which might counterfeit charity,
they were studious of works which might produce it.

> A brother said to Abba Sisoes, 'I am aware that
> the remembrance of God stays with me'. The old
> man said to him, 'It is no great thing to be with
> God in your thoughts, but it is a great thing to see
> yourself as inferior to all creatures.'[51]

Even if this recollection of God ($\mu\nu\acute{\eta}\mu\eta\ \theta\epsilon o\hat{v}$), celebrated as
it is, does not amount to much, more external heroics amount
to still less.

> Two brothers went to see a holy and solitary old
> man at Scetis. One of them said to him, 'Abba,
> I have learned the Old and New Testaments by
> heart'. The old man said to him, 'You have filled
> the air with words'. The other said, 'As for me,
> I have even copied out the Old and New Testaments
> from beginning to end, and I have them in my
> cell'. To this one he replied, 'As for you, you have
> filled your windows with parchments. Do you not
> know who said, "The kingdom of God does not
> consist in talk but in power?" (1 Cor 4:20). And
> again, "For it is not the hearer of the law who
> is righteous before God, but the doer of the law
> who will be justified" ' (Rom 2:13). They there-
> fore asked him for a way of salvation. He said to
> them, ' "The fear of the Lord is the beginning of

wisdom" (Ps 111:10), and humility with patience'.[52]

'Those who go to God have a great struggle, first exhaus-
tion and *then* ineffable joy. Those who wish to light a fire get
smoke in their eyes and shed tears; then they obtain the
desired result. We too must light the divine fire with tears
and hardship.'[53] The more one aspires to the love of God, the
more will one value this 'work'. Since perfection is without
end (ἀτέλεστος),[54] Mark the Hermit can attribute the same
quality to 'repentance', that is, the humility of believing
oneself a sinner. 'If one, under the pretext of acquired perfection, were to cease from practising the commandments
(which may be summed up in repentance), he would surely
stray from the true path.'[55] That is one danger to which the
true representatives of christian spirituality, especially in the
East, never expose themselves. Far from allowing the least
complacency over acquired perfection, they vie with each
other in repeating that they are only beginners, if indeed
they dare to give themselves even this title. When Abba
Sisoes was at the point of death, he had a vision. Questioned
by the brethren, he said:

'Look, the angels are coming to fetch me, and I am
begging them to let me do a little penance.' The
old men said to him, 'You have no need to do
penance, father.' But the old man said to them,
'Truly, I do not think I have even made a beginning
yet.' Now they all knew that he was perfect.[56]

Thus did they maintain that *penthos* from which they
expected everything.

It begins with charity itself. 'One of the fathers said, "All
work without humility is in vain. For humility is the precursor of charity. As John was the precursor of Jesus,
drawing all to him, so humility leads us to charity, that is to
God himself, since God is love".'[57] The author of the *Life* of
Saint Theognos tells us, 'I often saw this blessed man bathed
in tears and beseeching God for the entire world . . . . So he

often exhorted his disciples, saying, "If anyone does not
destroy the passions of the soul with the fire of such tears, he
will never be able to acquire charity, which is the fulness of
the law".'⁵⁸ It was indeed the love of God which caused
these holy men to weep; yet, in their conscious thought, this
was love desired rather than love possessed. I have never
found one who separated pure love from concern for his own
salvation. Such a view of spirituality they left to theologians.
In real life, charity is a living thing which begins with conversion, then is purified and grows toward unattainable perfection, always drawing nourishment from the same sap: the
grace of God and humble human sincerity. It is not accurate
to say that, for these authentic and primitive Christians,
concern for salvation prevailed over the impulse of pure love;
instead they showed their love by the earnestness with which
they applied it in practice. The heroes of the *Religious History*
left to Theodoret the task of writing a treatise to uncover the
secret spring of their exploits: 'divine and holy charity'.

Sometimes, though, despite their care to hide it, the inner
fire would throw some brightness outside. First are the
preachers, freer to rejoice in the sublime, supposing as they
did that no-one would suspect them of speaking of themselves or, even if they should want to be so suspected, that
no-one would be taken in. The best of them give themselves
away involuntarily. The *Lives* of Saint Ephrem and Saint
Theodore the Studite give guarantees of the sincerity of their
appeals to God's love to bring their hearers to compunction.
Other sayings sound like the admissions of children caught
redhanded.

> On the feast day after Easter, Palamon, the
> spiritual father of Pachomius, told him, "Because
> today is a christian holiday, rise and prepare
> breakfast for us'. And as he was preparing it, he
> put oil into the ground salt . . . . Pachomius invited
> him to eat. And when he came near what was
> prepared, he saw the oil in the salt; and striking

his face, he started crying, and said, 'The Lord has been crucified, and shall I eat oil?' And as Pachomius begged him fearfully, he barely agreed to sit down and eat, as was their custom, after the oil-dip had been emptied out. So was Palamon, the saint, always bearing the cross according to the Savior's word and following him with humble heart.[59]

One day when Abba Tithoes was sitting down, a brother happened to be beside him. Not realizing this, he began to groan, without thinking that the brother was beside him, for he was in ecstasy. Afterwards he made a prostration before him and said to him, 'Forgive me, brother; I have not yet become a monk, since I groaned in front of you.'[60]

When the same thing happened to John the Dwarf he said, 'Forgive me; I have not yet learned the catechism'.[61] The catechism of the spiritual life begins then by teaching the obligation of hiding one's virtuous deeds, and especially charisms. The great Macarius, invited one day to say 'a word to the brethren' in Abba Pambo's monastery, started his *fervorino* by saying, 'I have not yet become a monk myself, but I have seen monks'. Those incomparable ascetics whose feats he narrates had told him, 'If you cannot become like us, sit in your cell and weep for your sins'. He had kept this advice so well that

> if a brother came to see him with fear, like someone coming to see a great and holy old man, he did not say anything to him. But if one of the brethren said to him, as though to humiliate him, 'Abba, when you were a camel-driver, and stole nitre and sold it again, did not the keepers beat you?' If someone talked to him like that he would talk to them with joy about whatever they asked him.[62]

'Of the monks of Scetis it was said that if anyone caught sight of an observance, that is, came to know it, they would no longer hold it as a virtue, but as a sin.'[63]

A psychology like that does nothing to promote edifying biographies. To reveal the mystery of these extraordinary lives requires people indiscreet enough to peep through keyholes.

> A brother came to the cell of Abba Arsenius at Scetis. Waiting outside the door he saw the old man entirely like a flame. (The brother was worthy of this sight.) When he knocked, the old man came out and saw the brother marvelling. He said to him, 'Have you been knocking long? Did you see anything here?' The other answered, 'No'. So then he talked with him and sent him away.[64]

Poemen, the great hero of compunction, is no less heroic in his absolute silence about divine favors. Here again, a discreet confession opens up magnificent perspectives.

> Abba Joseph related that Abba Isaac said, 'I was sitting with Abba Poemen one day and I saw him in ecstasy and as I was on terms of great freedom of speech with him, I prostrated myself before him and begged him, saying, "Tell me where you were". He was forced to answer and he said, "My thought was with Saint Mary, the mother of God, as she wept by the cross of the Saviour. I wish I could always weep like that".'[65]

We do not know for certain whether Saint Anthony wept in this way, but we can infer it from one of the *Sayings*: 'Abba Anthony said, "I no longer fear God, but I love him, for love casts out fear".'[66] It is probably Saint Ammonas who preserved for us this astonishing confession[67]—astonishing, because it conflicts with everything we know from Saint Athanasius about the repeated 'flights of the man of God' to escape human esteem. Anthony did not even want the place of his burial known. Astonishing too must this statement

have seemed to later generations. Saint John Climacus seized
on it to support his theory of *apatheia*—he had so few others
to produce![68] Saint Dorotheos felt himself obliged to give
an exegesis of the text to prevent its being misunderstood.[69]
Indeed, we will never know very much, except by reasoning
in the manner of Theodoret, about the ardor with which the
hearts of our monastic ancestors burned for God. The
*Verba Seniorum* contains a section *De caritate* (V.17).
The disappointment we experience in turning to it only con-
firms this point. Except in numbers one and three, which
are the very sayings of Saint Anthony just mentioned, the
subject is simply fraternal charity. Paul Evergetinos, who
searched through the whole ascetic literature prior to his
time, found enough material for seven chapters on fraternal
charity.[70] They are drawn almost exclusively from the
*Sayings,* from Palladius, and from the *Life* of Saint Pachomius. On the love of God, there is just one chapter, thirteen
columns, taken from Mark the Hermit, Diadochus, Maximus
the Confessor, and Isaac the Syrian.[71] Only half a column
is taken from the *Geronticon,* four short anecdotes, three of
which go back again to Saint Anthony.[72]

Much later, a different spirit would appear in mystics like
Saint Symeon the New Theologian, whose teaching on tears
really deserves a separate study.[73] Here it is enough to note
three points:

First, it is indeed the love of God which causes Simeon
to pour out torrents, rivers, floods, streams, profusions,
masses of tears. This holy man was filled with tears, inun-
dated with them, he overflowed, he bathed the floor, he did
it as much while eating as while confessing and conversing
with God.[74] Most of the time these tears are sweeter than
honey.

Yet (and this is the second point) they are nonetheless
those of *penthos.* Even in his most exalted visions, the
enlightened one does not cease crying, 'Lord, have mercy on
me!'[75] This invocation was of course to have a tremendous

vogue, thanks chiefly to the Palamite hesychasts. One result of this, let it be noted in passing, is that hesychasm sank one of its roots in the traditional teaching on compunction.

Third, the New Theologian made a clean break with the law of silence concerning both flights of love and the charisms which inspire them. Symeon was perfectly aware of this rupture. (Isaac of Niniveh, although much more rarely, could also be 'foolish, . . . could not bear to keep the secret in silence'.[76]) It was his enemies who first forced him to abandon discretion. After that he became convinced that he had no right to bury the talent he had received. The ancients were of a different opinion, but it would not do to conclude from their reticence that their 'sorrowing' was any the less penetrated with the love of God.

# VI

## THE MEANS TO *PENTHOS*

SALVATION, PERFECTION, love of God and neighbor—
these are the elements which a Christian cannot afford
to neglect. Evidently, then, compunction is necessary for
all Christians. So Saint Gregory Nazianzen advises:

> Let everyone bring to God what fruits he can, at
> all times, at every turn of life and its events, to the
> measure of his ability according to the gifts he has
> been given . . . . Let one bring his goods, another
> the fact of having nothing; one his almsgiving,
> another the acceptance of alms; this one virtuous
> asceticism and that one a purified contemplation;
> this one a word in good season and that one a
> praiseworthy silence; one an impeccable teaching,
> another a willingness to learn; this one a spotless
> virginity which separates him from the world, that
> one an upright marriage which does not entirely
> separate him from God; one a fast without vain-
> glory, another a diet without intemperance; this
> one the absence of distraction at prayer and the
> office, that one the care of the needy. *Let everyone
> bring tears,* everyone purification, everyone pro-
> gress and constant striving toward improvement.[1]

'Let everyone bring tears' (πάντες δάκρυα) has a special force
here, because Gregory Nazianzen is one of the doctors who
do not accept the unity of virtue in the Stoic sense.[2]

Why is it that tears are so rare, even among those who
desire them and have experienced their ineffable sweetness?

53

Saint Athanasius answers this question:

> Not many have the gift of tears. Only those who
> keep their mind on the things above, who forget
> earthly things, who have no care for the flesh; who
> do not even know if there is a world, who have put
> to death their earthly members—to these alone is
> given the *penthos* of tears.[3]

To begin with, then, compunction is a gift of God. To forget
this is the best way to lose it.

> Even if you should weep fountains of tears in your
> prayer, do not exalt yourself inwardly. It is just
> that your prayer has been aided, so that you may
> generously confess your sins and appease the Lord
> with your tears. Do not then make a passion out
> of the remedy for passions, do not anger the Giver
> of grace. There are many who wept over their sins
> but forgot the purpose of tears. These have been
> taken in folly and have gone astray.[4]

Sometimes this grace acts for a specific reason, taking no
account of human dispositions. Someone had asked
Saint Basil,

> Why is it that sometimes, without effort, grief
> (πόνος) spontaneously overwhelms the soul and
> plunges it into compunction? Whereas at other
> times it is without grief (ἄπονος), unable to attain
> compunction even after doing violence to itself?'
> Reply: 'Compunction of this sort is a gift of God,
> either to awaken desire, so that the soul having
> once tasted the sweetness of this sorrow should
> strive to maintain it, or for showing that the soul
> with more serious application can remain in com-
> punction at all times and places, and so render
> inexcusable all who lose it through indolence.'[5]

If this is a grace, we must pray to obtain it.

> Without the help of grace the soul could never fill
> itself with compunction or confess its sins to the

Lord as it ought. Of itself it is weak and destitute
of all goods. Hateful and impure thoughts dwell
in it as an owl among the ruins. It is for man then
to invoke grace, that it may come and enlighten
his mind . . . and that he may consider the age to
come . . . . Tell me, my soul, why do you bathe
your face? . . . . If you wish to wash your face,
wash it, flood it with tears so that it may shine
with glory before God and his holy angels. A face
bathed with tears has an undying beauty.[6]

An example will show us how this prayer is heard. When
Melania the Younger and Pinianus wished to confer the
monastic habit on Gerontius,

they led him to the holy sepulchre of our Saviour
and placed different pieces of the *schema* [habit]
on the holy rock. Then they clothed him with these
as from the hands of our Lord, after asking for him
three things: upright faith, chastity, and tears. He
received all three, but especially the gift of tears.
Once ordained priest and having become *higoumen*
both of the monastery and the convents on the
holy Mount of Olives, he often celebrated three
liturgies on the same day, above all Sunday, one
on the holy mountain, one at the convent of men,
and one at the convent of women. On the other
days he celebrated a daily *synaxis* and a special
liturgy for the Blessed Melania, according to the
custom of the Roman Church. Now at each of
these *synaxes,* as soon as he had begun the sacred
liturgy, he wept until the very end, and with such
tears, sorrow, and compunction that none of
the faithful could contain himself. The whole
assembly would be filled with contrition, would
utter cries and groans and, like him, would
shed tears.[7]

Grace often makes use of outward events to overwhelm

the hardness of the human heart. The history of the Chosen
People is reenacted whenever Providence sends adversities to
bring sinners to repentance. No consideration has been more
used by preachers to awaken compunction. It is a truth
universally agreed on by them: calamities of all sorts have
no other ultimate reason than our sins. We have already
heard Saint Gregory Nazianzen, and could hear the same
from all the Doctors of the Church—John Chrysostom,
Gregory of Nyssa, Basil, to name only the most famous. But,
once again, it is Saint Ephrem who takes the prize for this
type of eloquence. He has his reasons for delighting in it,
among them the necessity of opposing the various dualistic
sects of his age. Marcionites, Bardesanians, Manicheans,
Messalians, all agreed that the origin of evil was to be sought
in a principle independent of the human will. They had to be
refuted by showing that free will is the sole source of all our
disorders. The misrule of liberty alone causes sin, and sin
draws the wrath of God which is manifested through natural
disasters. Ephrem did not hesitate to maintain that all
catastrophes—wars, floods, epidemics, famines—stem from
our backsliding. This is the theme of the first group of the
*Carmina Nisibina.* 'It is when you stop sinning that your
punishment will cease.'[8] The same certainty provided him
with ample material for sermons *de reprehensione, de
admonitione, de correctione,* wonderfully suited to touch
with compunction even the most hardened. Through these
terrible blows God takes it upon himself to give the shock—
the κατάνυξις—which causes tears to spring up, for the
salvation of those he loves.

Here we might well reread the homily of Saint Basil 'given
in time of famine and drought'. He would make us 'understand that it is because of our disdain and negligence that
God sends us these trials, not to beat us down but to raise us
up again'.[10] We are then exhorted to imitate the men of
Niniveh 'in mourning for their sins'. Let us not leave the business of praying just to innocent children who do not know

how, then, but rather, 'come, you who are soaked in sin, prostrate yourself, weep and moan, and leave the children to the amusements of their age'.

Severus of Antioch (who is no heretic in this matter) also gave homilies 'on correction'; for example, the one concerning 'the strange calamity sent by God to Alexandria'.[11]

> Those who suffer from this strange sickness bleat like sheep and goats, bark like dogs and utter other animal cries, feed on straw, grass and other animal food. All this is a fitting correction for our foolishness. So it is written: 'Man cannot abide in his pomp, he is like the beasts that perish' (Ps 49:12).[12]

God gives us up to these afflictions because

> we laugh at the threat of future punishment, we take no account of it, we hold the very name of Gehenna to be foolishness and deride hell itself as deserving no credence. Each of us says, 'As for me, I will enjoy the world which is near at hand and of short duration, and so I will arrive through my pleasures at the fire in which I will burn eternally. Yet it pleases me to seize visible enjoyment. As for fables of the invisible future, I care nothing for them.'[13]

It is then that the avenging arm intervenes to make us care. 'Let us be ashamed and correct ourselves . . . let us weep over ourselves . . . . Now let us use ardent and constant prayer . . . . But let us pray with tears, bending our knees to earth.'[14]

Alas, this sermon had little success. The following one complains that despite the threat of seeing the scourge, 'now headed for other cities', fall on them, the Christians of Antioch would still go from church to 'the diabolical spectacle of hippodrome and theatre'.[15] Still, Antioch was far from Alexandria, and we all cherish the secret hope that such things will happen only to others. In this same Antioch,

Saint John Chrysostom had once been able to congratulate
his hearers on the tears they shed and on their reformed
lives, but that was after an earthquake had shaken their own
city.[16]

Although heavy blows are needed to move the frivolous,
it is quite another matter for 'those who wish to be saved'.
Certainly, if it became necessary, rather than risk any
relaxation, all would imitate that 'brother of the Cells who
had reached such humility that he always said this prayer:
"Lord, send me a thunderbolt, for when I am well I disobey
you".'[17] If ever calamity struck them, they would certainly
imitate Saint Arsenius: 'When Scetis was destroyed he left
weeping and said, "The world has lost Rome and the monks
have lost Scetis".'[18] But these scourges were not necessary
and, in the long run, seem to have become less and less effec-
tive. The source, one often tapped by preachers, of temporal
punishments for sin may draw us to the desert, but there it
thins out and becomes imperceptible. What catastrophe would
be feared by men who had had the prowess to confront
demons in their own dwelling?

> One of the Fathers asked Abba Sisoes, 'If I am
> sitting in the desert and if a barbarian comes to
> kill me and if I am stronger than he, shall I kill
> him?' The old man said to him, 'No, leave him to
> God. In fact, whatever the trial is which comes to
> a man, let him say, "This has happened to me
> because of my sins," and if something good comes
> say, "It is through the providence of God".'[19]

As another saying has it, echoing the gospel, *Ne affligatur in
tribulatione. Ne timeat mortem, sed Deum.*[20]

*Si fractus illabatur orbis, impavidum ferient ruinae!*
Theodore of Pherme was no reader of Horace. It is neither
a Stoic theory nor a pedant's citation when he declares,
'If the sky should fall to the earth, Theodore will not fear'.
For, adds the narrative, 'he had asked God to remove from
him all cowardice.'[21]

Freed thus from human terrors, the solitary will still not lack outer stimuli for his *penthos*. Shielded from earthly fears, his sensitivity will be all the quicker to react to the slightest religious suggestion, whether in words or deeds. Apophthegmatic literature owes its existence to this frame of mind. What in other men causes spite and resentment will, in the ascetic, reawaken awareness of his faults. 'Abba Or taught this: in all temptations, do not complain about anyone else, but say about yourself, these things happen to me because of my sins.'[22] Even the shortcomings he observes will cause him to lament his own weakness. 'A holy man, seeing someone do evil, wept and said, "This one today, and surely myself tomorrow".'[23] He was only applying the principle of Abba Moses: 'It is folly for a man who has a dead person in his house to leave him there and go to weep over his neighbor's dead.' The devil himself nourishes compunction, as Abba Moses also teaches: 'In all temptations and evil thoughts, a man should weep and implore the goodness of God to come to his aid.'[24] The devil's henchmen unwittingly render the same service:

> Athanasius, archbishop of Alexandria of holy memory, begged Abba Pambo to come down from the desert to Alexandria. He went down, and seeing an actress he began to weep. Those who were present asked him the reason for his tears, and he said, 'Two things make me weep: one, the loss of this woman; and the other, that I am not so concerned to please God as she is to please wicked men.'[25]

The grace of God is thus offered on all sides. If the soul is humble and unattached, everything, good and evil, in it or in others, will be turned to compunction. A disciple of Saint Pachomius, Silvanos, wept to see himself, a sinner, served by saints.[26] Material necessities cause souls to groan, wishing to forget they have a body. The sacrosanct law of hospitality ordained that the host partake of the meal served to strangers, but 'it was said of Abba Poemen that if he was invited to eat

against his will, he wept but he went, so as not to refuse to
obey his brother and cause him pain'.[27] Enough on this
point. It begins to be evident that, through the grace of God,
*penthos* can indeed last forever.

This grace of God, nevertheless, requires our cooperation.
Such is the price of salvation, and so too of *penthos:* 'A
brother said to Abba Anthony, "Pray for me." The old man
said to him, "I will have no mercy on you, nor will God
have any, if you do not make an effort yourself and if you
do not pray to God".'[28] There are, then, two principal
means for awakening and maintaining compunction: examination of conscience and meditation. Without undertaking
a formal study of these practices in christian antiquity, we
merely point out that one of their *raisons d'être,* and not
the least, was the necessity of maintaining compunction.
Evagrius says, 'The beginning of salvation is to condemn
oneself,' and in the same lapidary style, Ephrem writes,
'The beginning of *penthos* is to know oneself!'[29] γνῶναι =
καταγνῶναι. The same affirmation may be formulated nega-
tively as: only those who do not know themselves do not
mourn. Even some holy men are in this state, such as the
good Mano, of whom we read in the *Life* of Saint Pachomius.[30] Pachomius had, as usual, given a catechesis full of
'many precautions for salvation'. Mano found that he exaggerated. 'Why is the old man recommending so many precautions to us? Are we about to fall every hour?' This, notes
the biographer, was because, 'not knowing the enemy's cun-
ning against souls, he felt himself safe'. The result: instead
of compunction, paralyzing grief—λυπούμενος. Mano remained
sleeping in his cell instead of accompanying his brothers in
cutting reeds. In the midst of all this, the 'Father of the
monastery' arrived, and Mano arose to meet him with others.
An expert in diagnosing both faces and hearts, Pachomius
lost no time in discerning the temptation and in rectifying
the error which was its cause. He needed nothing more than a
text of scripture: 'We all err in many matters' (Jm 3:2). He

might well, with Saint Ephrem,[31] have recalled the brusque statement of the beloved disciple: 'If we say we have no sin, we deceive ourselves, and the truth is not in us . . . . We make God a liar' (1 Jn 1:8,10). This blindness to self generally develops into harshness toward the faults of others.

A brother questioned Abba Poemen in this way, 'My thoughts trouble me, making me put my sins aside and concern myself with my brother's faults.' The old man told him the following story about Abba Dioscoros: 'In his cell he wept over himself, while his disciple was sitting in another cell. When the latter came to see the old man he asked him, "Father, why are you weeping?" "I am weeping over my sins," the old man answered him. Then his disciple said, "You do not have any sins, Father." The old man replied, "Truly, my child, if I were allowed my sins, three or four men would not be enough to weep for them".'[32]

Ἐὰν ἀφεθῶ ἰδεῖν: 'If I were allowed to see'. God has indeed allowed the saints to see, and they have not refused to look. Then, 'let us not be surprised to hear them weep,' as Saint Pachomius said to Saint Theodore. Since we are their children, let us instead imitate them by weeping first for ourselves, and then for our neighbor.[33] 'Which of them,' writes Saint Horsiesios, 'has not walked the road of this world in mourning and affliction?'[34]

It is through self-knowledge that sin itself can finally turn to the good of the sinner, thanks to the *penthos* which it inspires in him. One day Saint Pachomius spoke in high praise of one of his monks, without saying which one. Everyone began to conjecture: it is Theodore, it is Petronios, it is Horsiesios, all important men and future superiors. No, Pachomius finally admitted, it is Silvanos. This Silvanos had been an actor before becoming a monk. The first fervor of the novitiate having passed, he had fallen back into the ways of his first profession, softness and insolence. 'He would even repeat without fear, in the midst of the brothers, the unsuitable words of the stage.' On the point of being expelled from the community he asked for mercy, and Pachomius gave in, after publicly putting him through a merciless examination of conscience. When he had come to his senses, Silvanos became a model of compunction. 'The more he struggles, the more unworthy he holds himself. He wholeheartedly and sincerely believes himself a wretched good-for-nothing. His ease in shedding tears comes from this, that he truly thinks nothing of himself.'[35]

The *Life* of Saint Hypatius of Constantinople tells more briefly of a similar incident. A recently baptized 'scholastic' had such compunction that 'praying and weeping night and day, he brought us to compunction as well. He was of such a humble mind that he held himself to be the last of all.'[36] Here the biographer puts the cart before the horse. It is the sincerity of a low opinion of oneself which predisposes one to the gift of tears (and the writer of the *Life* expressly teaches that it is a gift). This humble opinion or persuasion, or better yet this frank disavowal of all superiority, this honest willingness to have no-one below oneself, this renunciation of the secret pleasure of having someone to look down on—all this can only come from an examination of conscience seriously carried out in the light of God.

Belief in the necessity of perpetual compunction was itself the cause of self-examination. The question put to Saint Basil—why do some have compunction and others not?[37]—must have bothered more than one conscience. It is no coincidence that we find it among the first of the *Short Rules,* the sixteenth out of three hundred thirteen. We find it repeated in the *Geronticon.* A brother who had the gift of tears to a superior degree (to the point of seeing a sign of his approaching death) was asked, 'Why do tears sometimes come of themselves, and sometimes cannot be produced even with great effort?' Saint Basil replied:

If we do not succeed in finding compunction, even despite violent efforts, this shows the negligence we have had at other times. We cannot obtain these things as though in passing, but only with application, with many and assiduous [one MS says 'uninterrupted'] exercises. This also shows that the soul is dominated by other passions which will not let it go freely toward what it desires, as the Apostle says, 'I am carnal, sold under sin . . . . For I do not do what I want, but I do the very thing I hate'. And again, 'It is no longer I who do it, but sin which dwells within me'. God allows this to happen to us, thus giving the soul a means of understanding its slavery through the things it suffers against its will. It understands itself in matters where it is the involuntary slave of sin, and can thus arouse itself to escape the devil's traps, finding God's mercy always ready to support the efforts of sincere repentance.[38]

Such failures serve as a warning which calls for an examination of conscience, provided of course that one believe in the necessity of compunction.

Of these passions which war against compunction, 'there are many in the soul of which we know nothing, until temptation comes and reveals them to us. We must then keep our hearts with great attention.'[39] That is why the spiritual teachers recommend examination of conscience so highly. 'The Fathers have taught us how each one must scrutinize himself (ἐξετάζειν ἑαυτόν),' says Saint Dorotheos in an instruction entitled, 'On cutting off passionate desires'. Bouts of fever may come and go, but a seven-day 'flu can leave us weak for months on end. We have agreed that *penthos* requires a vigorous soul. Whence comes our sickness? It is not for lack of knowledge in the physician, for Christ knows all things. Nor is it for lack of appropriate remedies since, for each passion, he has assigned the correct antidote. It is only our lack of restraint which allows passions to grow. If we had watched over them in time, they would not have sprung up to the point of choking compunction in us.[40]

There is no better way of shaking off this drowsiness than by meditation on the last things. Here is another subject which deserves a separate historical study; for now, just this remark: It would be quite contrary to the truth to suppose that the founders of recent Orders, in setting aside an hour for meditation, were introducing a new element into religious practice. What is new is not meditation but only its limitation to a set time. The ancient ascetics meditated always, or at least they were supposed to. They were certainly able to, having carefully eliminated all occupations incompatible with this exercise. Manual labor, reading, and psalmody would not distract their thoughts, as do the more or less secular studies required by the needs of the apostolate. The evolution in the practice of meditation stems from the evolution of religious life itself. The solitaries and cenobites of old could spread meditation out over a whole day. Preachers and teachers of today are forced to condense it into an hour. It is not that the ancients were unaware of meditation; it is just that the moderns have shortened it.

This may be obvious in the case of the hermits, but what of the cenobites? The Rule of Saint Pachomius never tires of repeating the recommendation: *de Scripturis aliquid meditari.*

36: Let him who calls the brethren meditate as he tolls.

37: Let him who gives dessert to the brethren at the refectory door meditate on something from Scripture as he gives it.

38: Returning to their cells, or going to the refectory, let all meditate on something from the Scriptures.

In order to insure the possibility of this meditation, the Pachomian rule contains a prescription which is surprising for its time and place.

139: If someone has entered the monastery without knowing how to read, then at the first, the third and the

sixth hour he shall go to someone who can teach him . . . .
The elements of syllables, verbs and nouns shall be written
for him, and even if he is unwilling, he shall be forced to
learn how to read.

140: And there shall be absolutely no-one in the monastery who has not learned to read and who does not know
something of the Scriptures, at least the whole New Testament and the Psalter.[41]

This requirement—to know certain sacred books and even
some spiritual writings by heart—will always endure. Thus
was perpetual meditation provided for.

What subjects should one prefer? Clearly, those most important to salvation, since the ascetic life has no other goal.

Abba Evagrius said, 'Sit in your cell, collecting
your thoughts. Remember the day of your death.
See then what the death of your body will be; let
your spirit be heavy, take pains, condemn the
vanity of the world, so as to be able to live always
in the peace you have in view without weakening.
Remember also what happens in hell and think
about the state of the souls down there, their
painful silence, their most bitter groanings, their
fear, their strife, their waiting. Think of their grief
without end and the tears their souls shed eternally. But keep the day of resurrection and of
presentation to God in remembrance also. Imagine
the fearful and terrible judgement. Consider the
fate kept for sinners, their shame before the face
of God and the angels and archangels and all men,
that is to say, the punishments, the eternal fire,
worms that rest not, the darkness, gnashing of
teeth, fear and supplications. Consider also the
good things in store for the righteous: confidence
before the face of God the Father and His Son, the
angels and archangels and all the people of the
saints, the kingdom of heaven, and the gifts of

that realm, joy and beatitude. Keep in mind the remembrance of these two realities: Weep for the judgement of sinners, afflict yourself for fear that you too feel those pains. But rejoice and be glad at the lot of the righteous. Strive to obtain those joys but be a stranger to those pains. Whether you be inside or outside your cell, be careful that the remembrance of these things never leaves you, so that, thanks to their remembrance, you may at least flee wrong and harmful thoughts.[42]

It is remarkable that of the many writings of Evagrius, only this one has been placed in the *Sayings of the Fathers,* apart from six other short sayings, of which one (no. 4) says, 'Always keep your death in mind and do not forget the eternal judgement, then there will be no fault in your soul'. This particular meditation, then, was read by innumerable monks and seculars. Note the strange reference to the tears shed by souls. The underlying thought is this: we can choose between bodily tears in this life and the far more bitter tears of the next life. To say this is only to interpret 'Blessed are those who weep' in conjunction with 'Woe to you who laugh now, for you shall mourn and weep.' (Lk 6:21,25) When Saint Poemen praises Saint Arsenius for having wept over himself in this world, he is careful to add the reason: 'He who does not weep for himself here below will weep eternally hereafter; so it is impossible not to weep, either voluntarily or when compelled through suffering.'[43] Saint Gregory of Nyssa writes:

There are two lives and two ways to follow in each of these lives taken separately. There are even two joys, one in this life and the other in that for which we hope. What then is blessed? That we should reserve our share of joy for the true goods of eternal life, and accomplish our service of sadness in this short and fleeting life. We regret not the loss of any of our temporal pleasures, but rather the loss of greater joys because of our enjoyment of these lesser ones. If then we may call happy the possession of an endless joy stretching across infinite ages, and if human nature must unavoidably taste as well what is opposed to joy, there is no longer any difficulty in understanding the reason for this saying, 'Blessed are those who mourn now, for they will be comforted in endless ages'.[44]

Abba Moses said, 'When we have succumbed to a corporal passion, let us not neglect repentance and mourning over ourselves, lest the mourning of the judgement should seize us.'[45]

Saint Ephrem could not fail to insist on this point: 'Let us weep a little in this life, so as not to have to weep eternally in the tortures of the next . . . . At the hour of judgement you will groan bitterly and you will shed tears, but to no avail. Therefore, have pity on yourself in the present.' Meditate on the mourning of those who have laughed in this world, and the joy of those who have wept.[46]

When one's mind is taken up with an idea, almost any object will serve to recall it. Saint Macarius found a skull in the desert and heard, or thought he heard, a whole sermon on the pains of hell.[47] It took very little to inspire thoughts of the last end of those for whom this meditation was the chief concern.

A fervent brother came from abroad and dwelt in a small cell on Mount Sinai. On the day of his arrival he found a small wooden tablet left by the brother who had dwelt there. It bore this inscription: 'Moses to Theodore, I am present and I attest'. He took this tablet and each day he put it before his eyes, questioning as if the writer were present: 'Where then are you, O man who say that you are present and that you attest? In what world or in what place are you? Where is the hand

which wrote that?' He did this all day, remembering death, ceaselessly shedding tears. As his work
was calligraphy, he received from the brothers
parchments and orders for writing, but he died
without having written a word. He had simply
noted on each one's parchments, 'Forgive me,
masters and brothers, but I was busy with someone
and because of that I had no time to write
for you.'[48]

The smallest events of daily life lead to the same reflections:

An old man met one of the seated fathers
[=hesychasts] at Raithou and said to him, 'Abba,
when I send the brother who is with me to some
task I worry, especially if he delays in returning.'
The old man replied, 'As for me, when I send my
servant to some labor, I sit near the door and I look
out. And when my thoughts say to me, "Will the
brother ever come back?" I say in turn to my
thoughts, "And what if another brother comes
before him to send me to the Lord, an angel, what
then?" And so I remain seated each day, watching
the door, meditating and weeping for my sins and
saying, "Which of the two brothers will come first,
the one from on high or the one from below?" '
The old man went away touched with compunction, and from that time he adopted the same
practice.[49]

Abba Theophilus the archbishop [of Alexandria],
at the point of death, said, 'You are blessed, Abba
Arsenius, because you have always had this hour
in mind'.[50]

The greatest of the cenobiarchs seem to have feared that
their monks might have illusions concerning the certainty of
their salvation. If this were the case, then it mattered
nothing that the monastic life was sublime, the religious

profession a kind of sacrament which remits sins and gives
the Holy Spirit, the *schema* holy and angelic. What all must
meditate, 'be they courageous or dismayed, great or small,
fervent or lukewarm, rich or poor in virtue, every man be he
from among us or from without [=monk or secular], from
every tribe and every tongue'—all must consider the great
truths of human destiny. Theodore the Studite returned to
this theme in nearly all his catecheses; in the one just cited
he shows that he has read and nearly memorized the passage
of Evagrius in the *Sayings*.[51] Theodore was a champion of
tradition and, if his preaching were any different, would
have been afraid of betraying the Gospel itself. He was also
very familiar with Saint Pachomius, the father of cenobites.[52]
And 'our father Pachomius was perfect in everything, but
austere and always in mourning ($\pi\epsilon\nu\theta\eta\rho\eta\varsigma$); he reminded
one of the souls given over, like Dives, to punishments.'[53] It
comes as no surprise, then, to hear this stern preacher of the
last things propose as the ideal monk Silvanos, with his
uncontrollable tears:

> His great superiority in virtues came from his
> extreme humility and the inexhaustible richness of
> his eyes in shedding tears—to the point that, even
> when eating with his brothers, he could not master
> his tears, but mingled them with his pittance. When
> his brothers told him not to do that before
> strangers, he would assure them, 'I have often
> tried to withhold my tears for that very reason,
> but I could not . . . I weep, therefore, brothers,
> because I fear being swallowed up like Dathan and
> Abiram, all the more so since, having come from
> ignorance to the knowledge of God, I have not
> care for the salvation of my soul . . . That is why
> I am not ashamed to behave this way.'[54]

Another Silvanos appears in the *Sayings* as head of a colony
of hermits in Sinai. One of his sayings had an undying fame
in monastic circles: 'Unhappy is the man whose reputation

is greater than his work.'[55] This man was an ecstatic, and the authenticity of his visions is guaranteed by the fact that he was at the same time an opponent of the Messalians. Now

> as he was sitting with the brethren one day he was rapt in ecstasy and fell with his face to the ground. After a long time he got up and wept. The brethren besought him saying, 'What is it, father?' But he remained silent and wept. When they insisted on his speaking he said, 'I was taken up to see the judgement and I saw there many of our sort coming to punishment and many seculars going into the kingdom.' The old man was full of compunction and never wanted to leave his cell. If he was obliged to go out, he hid his face in his cowl saying, 'Why should I seek to see this earthly light, which is of no use?'[56]

I cannot refrain from citing here some lines from an author who studied the characteristics of primitive monasticism without any concern for modern synthesis, Karl Heussi:

> The third saying of Dioscoros[57] shows the extent to which monastic life was determined by fear of the last judgement, the fear of not having a wedding garment and of being found naked after wearing the monastic habit for so long, of the darkness which might fall on the monk condemned in the eyes of the fathers and brothers, who would see the monks condemned to hell being tortured by the angels of punishment. This text receives a particularly interesting development in the two Colbertine codices: 'What sadness will overcome Abba Anthony, Abba Ammonas of Nitria, Abba Paul of Phoca, Abba Ammonas of Arabia in Egypt, Abba Mios of the Thebaid, Abba Macarius of Scetis, Abba Macarius of Alexandria, Paphnutius Sindomas, Abba Orseres of Thegoua, Abba Ammonias of

Cheneurita, and all the other just men when they are admitted to the kingdom of heaven while we are thrown into outer darkness?[58] This is the greatest shame that a monk can expect, not to be found a true monk in the eyes of those who were true monks. The fear of God and the fear of eternal damnation are closely united in this concept, one that is chiefly eschatological, just as they were united in primitive Christianity. It is because, when one fears God one fears Him who can cast soul and body into Gehenna.[59]

It is of course because the monks took these fundamental truths so seriously and meditated on them so earnestly that the truths in turn inspired the monks with so much compunction. As Saint John Chrysostom puts it, 'When tears come from the fear of God they last forever'.[60] Conversely, it was because they desired compunction so strongly that the ascetics, far from avoiding such austere points of meditation, took them up in preference to others which were less helpful.

There is an exercise which in a sense combines the advantages of examination of conscience with those of meditation, and adds the particular grace of obedience. This is the opening of one's soul to a spiritual father, the famous *exagoreusis*. The subject is too vast to do more than mention here. The principle of it was enunciated by Saint Anthony himself: 'If he is able to, a monk ought to tell his elders confidently how many steps he takes and how many drops of water he drinks in his cell, in case he is in error about it.'[61] Even the love of silence cannot withstand this necessity. What is instead required is ἀσιώπητον, which is as Saint Barsanuphius explains, 'never to keep silent one's own thoughts'.[62] It is partly because of this law that eremitism finally failed. Such 'confession' is barely conceivable without tears or, if it is done with no trace of feeling, one can conclude that it is worth very little.

Two brothers who lived separately met each other.

One said, 'I will go to Abba Zeno and submit my thoughts to him'. The other said, 'I will do the same'. They therefore went together. Each in turn presented himself and opened his thoughts. The first made his confession by prostrating himself before the old man and begging him with many tears to pray for him. The old man said to him, 'Go, do not be discouraged. Say no evil of anyone and do not neglect your prayer'. The brother went his way and was healed. The other, having spoken his thoughts to the old man, added weakly and carelessly, 'Pray for me'. He did not however ask earnestly. Some time later the two brothers met, and one said to the other, 'When we went to the old man, did you manifest the thoughts to him which you said you wanted to confess?' 'Yes,' he said. The other then asked, 'Did it help you to tell him that?' The brother replied, 'Yes, through the old man's prayers God has healed me'. The other said, 'As for me, it did me no good to open myself, I have not felt any effects of the cure'. The one who was healed answered him, 'And how did you beseech the old man?' He said, 'I said to him, "Pray for me, because I have these thoughts".' 'And I,' said the first, 'while making my confession, I bathed his feet with my tears, begging him to pray for me, and through his prayers God has restored to me my health.'[63]

If confiding one's thoughts to a man of God aids compunction, what may we not expect from the reply the man will give? This reply, after all, will be the reply of the Spirit. The point was perfectly understood by Dom Ildephonsus Herwegen in his short but excellent work *Väterspruch und Mönchsregel*.[64] Even a secular writer like Heussi could recognize the divinely-inspired quality attributed to the sayings.[65] For that matter, we find the doctrine not only

presupposed throughout the whole apophthegmatic literature, but still being explicitly affirmed long afterwards. Only
a false scepticism would deny it today. Nothing could be
clearer on this point than the repeated affirmations of
Saint Barsanuphius. For example, in writing to a 'professor
of worldly wisdom', he says,

> Reflect. You are a professor of worldly wisdom
> and you have pupils. If then you dictate a letter to
> one of them, will your pupil write what you want,
> or will he leave that to write whatever he wants?
> Clearly, he will write what you tell him and not
> what he wants. Even so, the saints do not speak
> from within themselves, but God speaks in them as
> he wishes, sometimes enigmatically, sometimes
> clearly. To convince you that it is so, the Lord
> himself said to his disciples, 'It is not you who
> speak but the Spirit of your Father who speaks in
> you.' (Mt 10:20) So then, he speaks as he will, and
> not as they will . . . . Go, take heed to yourself, and
> pray that God may give you a firm heart and an
> unshakeable faith. And do not be scandalized by
> the saints, for the spirit which speaks in them
> makes no mistake. In them is the word of Scrip-
> ture fulfilled, 'Let thy good spirit lead me on a
> level path.' (Ps 143:10)[66]

Barsanuphius defended the idea of infallible inspiration
against all objections, sometimes using amazingly subtle
arguments. When two old men reply differently to the same
question it is because between the two interrogations the
listener changed his attitude, as did King Hezekiah between
the two messages of Isaiah, or the Ninevites between Jonah's
threat and its revocation.[67] If a reply does not produce the
desired effect, the blame lies solely with the faulty dispositions of the disciple.[68]

'Whoever asks the Fathers fulfills the Law and the
prophets.'[69] He will necessarily have compunction as well,

since it is commanded by the new decalogue, the Beatitudes.
'An old man said "The Lives and the sayings of the old men
enlighten the soul, filling it with spiritual tears".'[70] There are
abundant examples to show this effectiveness: some have
already been cited in the section on *catanyxis*. More can be
found in Saint Barsanuphius' letters: 'An old man, having
received one of his letters, gave himself up to mourning and
tears for many days,' so much so that the great elder wrote
him again to console him. The first of these letters did not
in fact contain anything very upsetting—but how could one
avoid being shaken, seeing that one's spiritual father had the
gift of discerning hearts?[71] This teaching will find its comple-
tion in the section on obstacles to compunction.

Liturgy should clearly have a place of honor in a chapter
devoted to the means for arriving at compunction. It is the
*Opus Dei* at the heart of that ἔργον τοῦ θεοῦ which is, for
Saint Anthony, the whole of the ascetic life.[72] It gathers
within itself all the effectiveness of other exercises. 'The
praise of the psalms is a lament,' said the father of monasticism, and a variant of this saying makes it hold true for all
Scripture.[73] The earliest Divine Office was made up entirely
of scriptural readings, chiefly of psalms. Canticles did not
appear until later—and we shall soon have a word to say
about them. To psalmodize is to meditate (μελετᾶν ψαλμούς,
it was said); it is to pray, it is to examine oneself, as we have
already seen;[74] it is thus to put oneself in the best possible
state for obtaining *penthos*. If the Fathers do not say this
more often it is because for them the truth is self-evident.
Anyone who doubts it has only to compare their incessant
seeking after compunction with their earnest application
to psalmody.

Diadochus tells us, with his accustomed finesse, what
sort of psalmody is the most conducive to tears:

> When the soul abounds in its natural state it gives
> itself to psalmody with a louder voice and prefers
> vocal prayer. But when it is under the action of the

Holy Spirit it sings softly and quietly, and it prays only from the heart. From the first disposition comes a joy of the imagination. From the second come spiritual tears and, after a while, a sense of contentment with silence. Recollection is then kept warm, thanks to the moderation of the voice, and so prepares the heart to conceive thoughts which are peaceful and conducive to tears. In this way we can really see the seeds of prayer sown in the heart's earth in the hope of a good harvest. In the meantime, whenever we are weighed down by great desolation we must psalmodize with a slightly stronger voice, stimulating the soul with the joy of hope until the heavy cloud is dispersed by the wind of melody.[75]

Such are the ordinary means which everyone must follow: examination of conscience, meditation on the last things, *exagoreusis*. It is hard to suppose that these would not be more than enough. Nevertheless, it can happen that the heart stubbornly refuses to the eyes the soft rain of tears. The fault for this, Saint Basil tells us sharply, lies in previous negligence. The great master of asceticism has spoken; who would dare contradict? Besides, the Fathers had no desire to advance theories which would remove opportunities for self-blame and then perhaps for a restoration of *penthos*. Yet there was one—he remained anonymous—who seems to have hazarded a more indulgent view. Although himself extraordinarily gifted with the charism of tears, he appears to be unusually competent on this point:

'Why do tears sometimes come of themselves, but sometimes only with great effort?' The old man replied, 'Tears are like rain, and man is the farmer. He who cultivates the earth of his heart must, when they come, use every device to lose nothing of this rain. He must see that all goes into his garden. For I tell you, my children, often there is only one day

of rain at the beginning of the entire year, but he
saves his whole crop. That is why we must take care
and try to watch over ourselves, praying earnestly
to God, for we know not if we will again have
another day of rain like this'.[76]

This text had to be given for the sake of honesty. One
cannot say *conclamant Patres* while there remains one dis-
cordant voice. Some reflections on this dissonance will
follow, but now a practical question remains. What is to be
done in case of dryness, and how can it be prevented from
lasting too long? Generally speaking, the best answer seems
to be that all means are good, even the least expected, and
even some which may appear suspect. This serves to remind
us not to be misled when everything seems easy. Compunction, like the whole spiritual life, requires κόπος, hard labor.
'It is in piercing the heart that the monk brings forth tears.'
'Tears wash away sins. They come through κόπος, through
great application and endurance, through meditation on the
terrible judgement and eternal confusion, through self
denial . . . . To deny oneself and to take up one's cross means
cutting off one's will and its claims.'[77] Our first recourse then
should be to a more generous self-denial.

Secondly, we must create a favorable ambiance. This will
consist primarily of two elements: poverty and solitude. 'If
you wish to acquire *penthos,* watch carefully to see that all
your clothes and the things you use are as poor as those of
our brethren who sit in public places begging alms.'[78] In one
MS this recommendation is followed by a fragment whose
conclusion one would like to know. It begins, 'If you own a
book, do not decorate the binding . . . ' .[79] The series
continues:

He also said, 'In your cell, your hands must not
even touch an object of silver or gold, however
small. I mean that not only must you not wish to
touch an object of this sort sent to you for some
task, not even if it is a small cross or anything like

it made of gold or silver.' Again he said, 'Do not
hang a knife from your belt, for that sort of thing
prevents compunction. Your bedcover, your
clothes, your shoes, your belt, and all your
things must be such that thieves who come to take
them will find nothing to please them among
these objects or any that are in your cell.'[80]

The Berlin MS contains several other pieces of advice of this
sort; they must have been part of a small treatise on compunction. It all comes to this: if you want to have the consolation of *penthos,* you must renounce all pleasures of
ownership.

Solitude must also be cultivated, and with it the renunciation of distractions. We are driven to these by *accedia,* and
we know that *accedia* drives away tears. It is no accident that
Saint Arsenius is a great example of both compunction and
the flight from men. 'Flee, be silent, pray always,' an angel
said to him after he had already obeyed a previous order to
flee from men.

Abba Mark said to Abba Arsenius, 'Why do you
avoid us?' The old man said to him, 'God knows
that I love you, but I cannot live with God and
with men.'[81]

Blessed Archbishop Theophilus, accompanied by a
magistrate, came one day to find Abba Arsenius.
He questioned the old man, to hear a word from
him. After a short silence the old man answered
him, 'Will you put into practice what I say to
you?' They promised him this. 'If you hear Arsenius is anywhere, do not go there.'[82]

According to one monk, the reason why succeeding generations have lost the *penthos* of the ancients is that they have
not kept their love of recollection and poverty:

A brother asked an old man, 'How is it, Father,
that our generation cannot maintain the *ascesis* of

the Fathers?' The old man replied, 'Because it does
not love God, does not flee from men [compare
Saint Arsenius!], and does not hate the material
goods of this world. To the man who flees from
men and hates material goods, compunction comes
of itself, and *ascesis* as well. One cannot put out a
fire in a field unless one begins by removing what
lies in its way. Unless a man goes to a place where
he will have difficulty even in finding bread; he
will not acquire *ascesis* [and so compunction].'[83]

Even for the hermits there are degrees of solitude. Wise
men tell us to use our hours of most perfect isolation to cultivate the 'garden of compunction'. This is the place to cite a
somewhat longer but very appealing story, one which has
practically never appeared in print:

One day a brother, about to leave for the city,
went to a brother who lived nearby and who had
continual compunction. He said to his fervent
neighbor, 'Please do me the kindness, brother, of
taking care of my garden until my return.' The
other replied, 'Believe me, brother, I will do my
best not to neglect it'. After the brother's depar-
ture he said to himself, 'Come on now, you have
the time, take care of the garden'. And from
evening to dawn he stood in psalmody, ceaselessly shedding tears. He prayed the same way for
the entire day. Coming home late, the brother
found that hedgehogs had ravaged his garden. He
said, 'God forgive you, brother, for not taking
care of my garden'. He answered, 'God knows,
Abba, I did my best to keep it and I hope through
God's mercy that the little garden will bear fruit'.
The brother said, 'Well, brother, it has been
completely destroyed'. The other replied, 'I know,
but I have confidence in God that it will flower
again'. The owner of the garden said, 'Come on,

let's water it'. The other said, 'You water it now, and I will water it at night'. When a drought came, the gardener said to his companion, 'Believe me, brother, if God does not come to our rescue, we will have no water this year'. The other answered, 'Woe to us, brother, if the springs of the garden dry up, then we will have no further chance of salvation'. But he spoke of tears and of the garden of his heart, watered by him and in full flower.[84]

The effect of solitude on *penthos* raised problems of conscience. When compunction comes, is that not the time to draw as much as possible from it, giving oneself solely to prayer in absolute retirement? A difficult question, to judge from the variety of solutions it received. The anonymous Father whose disagreement with Saint Basil's doctrine has already been noted also took up this question:

Again we asked him, 'How should we keep compunction, when it comes?' The old man replied, 'You must be sure to meet no-one on the day when *penthos* is acting. You must also keep yourself from greed and thoughts of pride. You must not even be sure that you are weeping, and judge no-one, but give yourself up to prayer and reading.'

And yet, there are surprises!

'I know a brother who was seated in his cell, busy with weaving, when *penthos* came to him. As his tears flowed he arose to pray, and immediately the tears ceased. He therefore went back to his weaving, recollecting his spirit, and soon the tears returned. The same thing happened while he was reading. Compunction came, but when he got up for prayer it disappeared. Then the brother recognized the cause of this difference and said to himself, "The fathers were right in saying that *penthos* is a master, for it teaches man all that he needs".'[85]

The solution is unclear and becomes even less clear when,

a little further on, another old man recommends putting
down one's manual labor when tears come. Explanations are
added. What a terrible thing if the reader were to suppose
that prayer is not in every case the most favorable occupation for *penthos!*

> 'I think that the brother lost *penthos* in prayer for
> two reasons. First, because his prayer was not yet
> pure and free from distractions. It was these which
> dispersed his thoughts and prevented him from
> keeping the compunction which he had had during
> manual labor and reading, when he was more
> recollected. [Does this mean that manual labor
> can therefore be more favorable to recollection
> than prayer?] Second, so that he might not ima-
> gine himself to have obtained *penthos* through his
> own efforts and prayer, but that he might recog-
> nize that this was given him by the mercy and
> grace of God. Thence he might be made grateful to
> God's generosity and so more humble, and through
> these dispositions *penthos* would acquire greater
> strength in him. But as for us, if ever such a thing
> should happen, that is, if compunction of heart
> and the warmth of tears should overcome us, let
> us immediately put aside all the rest and run to
> prayer. Let us persevere in that until we feel the
> fire of the heart burning in us, for who knows
> when we will again have the same abundance?'

These arguments do not hold up, either logically or patris-
tically. Why run to prayer *in order* to enjoy *penthos* if one
happens to find it more readily in manual labor? More im-
portantly, the author of these lines has forgotten that we are
forbidden to think ourselves better than others. The brother
did not have pure prayer but we, of course, have it and so
should not act like him. And then, have we less need of
learning thankfulness? If this opinion were really from an
ancient Father, Saint Barsanuphius would have known

it and would not have dared to give his own:

> A brother asked the great old man, 'Tell me,
> Father, if the compunction which I think I have is
> authentic, and if I should therefore remain apart?'

We will save the beginning of his reply until later; here is the
end:

> 'As for remaining apart, that would be presump-
> tion. When the moment [of perpetual compunc-
> tion] comes, I will tell you myself. In the
> meantime, my child, take pains, as I have told you,
> and I am confident that you will make progress
> in Christ.'[86]

Despite this disagreement on a secondary point, one idea
is common to all the spiritual teachers: the usefulness, the
necessity, of withdrawal for (to use a later expression)
finding grace. Hence the unending praises of the cell.
*Penthos* will teach us everything and so will our cell
because, when we keep to it unrelentingly, it will give us
*penthos.* One saying is repeated, like a verse of Scripture, by
the ascetics of all ages. 'It is said [this phrase usually intro-
duces scriptural citations], keep to your cell and your cell
will teach you everything.'[87] Isaac of Nineveh quotes the
saying with the same 'it is said'.[88] The words come from
Abba Moses,[89] but the advice itself goes back to no-one less
than Macarius the Great:

> Abba Isaiah questioned Abba Macarius saying,
> 'Give me a word'. The old man said to him, 'Flee
> from men'. Abba Isaiah said to him, 'What does it
> mean to flee from men?' The old man said, 'It
> means to sit in your cell and weep for your sins.'[90]

Abba Aïo received the same order: 'Flee from men, stay in
your cell, weep for your sins, do not take pleasure in the
conversation of men, and you will be saved.'[91] Only in his
cell is a monk in his element, as a fish is in water.[92] It is here,
therefore, that he will gain that *penthos* to which his vows
bind him. To leave not the slightest doubt as to the certainty

of this result, the *Sayings* recount the following incident, a
somewhat surprising one in that it sins somewhat against the
law of confidence in the Fathers:

> There was a brother who lived in the desert of the
> Thebaid and the thought crossed his mind, 'Why
> do you live here in this useless way? Get up and go
> to the monastery and there you will make progress.'
> So he went and found Abba Paphnutius and told
> him about this thought. The old man said to him,
> 'Go and stay in your cell; make only one prayer in
> the morning and one in the evening and one at
> night. When you are hungry, eat, and when you are
> thirsty, drink; when you are tired, sleep. But stay
> in the cell and take no notice of this thought.' The
> brother went and found Abba John and told him
> what Abba Paphnutius had said and Abba John
> said, 'Don't pray at all, just stay in the cell'. So the
> brother went and found Abba Arsenius and told
> him all about it and the old man said to him, 'Do
> as the others have told you. I have nothing to say
> but that', and he went away satisfied.[93]

One detects here an echo of the controversies concerning the
eremitical and cenobitic lives. Yet the fact that the last court
of appeal was Saint Arsenius shows also that the writer of this
text was thinking of the gift of tears.

Is it necessary to add that the founders of the common
life had not the slightest concern, as has been suggested, for
providing their cenobites with 'people to be with and things
to do'?[94] They felt simply that the 'flight from men' could
be realized even in community, through the law of silence.
The hermits themselves had understood this. 'Abba Poemen
said, "If you are silent, wherever you are you will find rest
(that is, the satisfaction of your spiritual desires)."[95] 'Abba
Tithoes used to say, "True *xeniteia* [flight from men] means
that a man should control his own tongue".'[96] 'Flee from
this,' said another, putting his finger over his mouth.[97]

Inasmuch as there is less solitude in monasteries than in colonies of anchorites—it is only a question of degree—the axiom of Abba Moses may be rendered thus: keep silence, and silence will teach you everything, and first, the beginning of all, compunction. One could also take as axiomatic, with no changes in wording, the saying of Poemen: 'The first time flee; the second time, flee; and the third, become like a sword.'[98] Απότομοι, trenchant as swords, were the great Fathers with nuisances whose chatter imperiled their *penthos.*

One could hardly expect all these means to take instant effect, yet there are moments when the need for compunction is so great that one must do more than just wait for it to come by and by. What is to be done then? Cassian, a Latin, has a low opinion of 'forced tears',[99] a point on which he differs from some of his Eastern brethren, notably the one he follows faithfully in other matters, Evagrius Ponticus.[100] 'At the beginning of prayer, force yourself to tears and compunction, so that your prayer may become fruitful.'[101] Is it enough, as it is for virtue in general, simply to desire it? This is the constant teaching of Evagrius' scholarly master, Saint Gregory Nazianzen.[102] The highly optimistic theory of the Greek Fathers concerning the power of free will seems to provide direction to Evagrius' thought on this point.[103] Were it otherwise, we might expect him to suggest some techniques for our use, and yet the only one I can remember having read in him is the one to be used in any temptation, *antirrhesis.* It is, for instance, a temptation to have 'a hardened soul which will not shed tears';[104] this is the temptation of *accedia.* It is to be opposed with a verse of Holy Scripture: 'I am weary with my moaning; every night I flood my bed with tears: I drench my couch with weeping'. (Ps 6:6) This is only an encouragement to desire tears, 'because the shedding of tears is a great remedy against the night visions which spring from *accedia,* and the prophet David applied this remedy to his passions when he spoke' this verse. David also said, 'My tears have been my food day and night'. (Ps 42:3). This phrase must be addressed to the soul which supposes that tears do no good in the struggle against *accedia*.[105] Evagrius does not contradict the master whose community he forsook, Saint Basil, who said that it is all our fault if we have no compunction. Our only recourse is to one of those 'catanyctic' prayers of which Evagrius has left us such a fine specimen in the *Paraneticon*.[106]

We must force ourselves. Even Evagrius' great opponent, Saint Barsanuphius, affirms the same thing, speaking through his *alter ego,* John the Prophet, in reply to the following question:

> 'The old man has told me that my present tears are not authentic, since they come and go. If so, then what state am I in? And must I force myself or be patient until true compunction comes?'
>
> 'Your present tears are not authentic, coming and disappearing, because your will is unstable, sometimes ardent. When ardor persists then compunction gains great stability, and from thence ensue tears. Take pains, then, and force tears to come. Brother, do not neglect to observe the recommendations and orders of the old man, and you will be saved.'[107]

'We *must* have *penthos*,' said Saint Poemen and several others. If it is a duty, then logic and conscience will dictate that we do it, by constraint, if need be.

*Penthos* is called 'pain' in the *Verba Seniorum*, sometimes πόνος by the Greeks, as in the passage of Saint Basil cited above.[108] One weeps when one is in pain. Starting from there, those who were impatient to shed tears could get the idea of obtaining them from voluntary sufferings. The hair-shirt, says Saint Basil, has as its goal mortification [ill-treatment, κακουχία] and humiliation of the soul.[109] The same should probably be said of fasting and all other sorts of κακουχίαι. These practices predispose us to compunction, but do not lead us to it instantly. Are there no more direct methods? To a brother who wanted to know 'how a man can come to weep', an old man told this story:

> I heard of a brother who renounced the world and went to live in the mountain of Nitria. His cell was situated near that of another brother. Every day he heard him constantly weeping for his sins. But when his tears were slow in coming he would say to his soul, 'You do not weep, wretch, you do not sob? Let me assure you that, if you will not, I will make you weep.' He would then arise, take a whip that he had which was made of a solid handle from which hung a double cord, and he would beat himself vigorously until, as a result of the pain, he began to weep.

This is such an unusual story that it requires heavenly approval:

> His neighbor was bewildered by these actions of his brother, and prayed that God might reveal to him if perhaps he was right in torturing himself. One night in a dream he saw this brother wearing a crown and standing in the choir of martyrs, and another said to him, 'See how this generous athlete who tortures himself for Christ has been crowned with the martyrs'.[110]

A deed of this kind is so rare (there are none in the alphabetical *Sayings*) that the writer had to take some precautions. All the characters are anonymous—the brother who questions, the elder who replies, the hero himself, the witness, and above all the sources, since all this is hearsay.

This flagellant will find occasional imitators, but he will have to wait a long time for them. The first that I know of is Saint Cyril of Philea in the eleventh century: 'While praying to God he made frequent genuflections, and then beat himself mercilessly on the thighs and shoulders, sometimes with a cord and sometimes with a stick of wood, and

sometimes even with a buckthorn . . . ' . We can stop there.
The flogging continues, with floods of tears obtained as
recompense for torrents of blood.[111] In the twelfth century
*Life* of Leontius, patriarch of Jerusalem, the monk Theodore
tells us that when Leontius presented himself at the monastery of Saint John the Evangelist at Patmos, he was denied
entrance into the community because of his still beard-
less face.

> The young man therefore remained in his cell,
> neglecting nothing in his exact observance of the
> monastic rule. His prayer was uninterrupted, as
> were his reading of the Holy Books, his psalmody
> and his zeal for virtues. As for tears, they flowed
> like streams from his eyes. Then, while the other
> brothers were sleeping, and when he could not
> easily weep, he had ready a lash with which he
> whipped his bare body, and from these pains he
> would weep even without wishing to. Numerous
> nails were attached to this lash, so that when he
> beat himself with them, his flesh was torn deeply
> and blood flowed. Thus he obtained violent suffer-
> ings for himself which caused him to shed bitter
> and hot tears . . . . To those who saw him he
> appeared all dried out and weakened. This was
> because of his whippings and wounds, although
> none knew the cause.[112]

We, of course, know it because his biographer has told us.
Such is the search for compunction by any and every means.

Could not these very rare 'athletes' (I have mentioned all
I know) be accused of lacking discretion in every sense?
Would the ancients have approved of this violent *ascesis*?
I think that they would have objected, just as did Saint
Theodore the Studite, who knew his *Geronticon* by heart:
'Where then has any one of the saints done such things?'[113]
As for those tears wrenched out by physical pain, have they
anything in common with compunction? Let us see. The

anonymous old man now continues, in the same passage:

I know of a brother who was eager for suffering. When his heart was hard he would often beat himself, and from intense suffering he would begin to weep. As soon as this happened, he would quickly think of the place of torment and of all his sins.[114]

There is the trick. If it is legitimate, how can one forbid others which are equally capable of success? The remembrance of relatives absent or deceased draws us naturally to mourning. Too naturally, the old masters would have said.[115] Such mourning has nothing to do with ascetic *penthos*, except perhaps as an enemy, through the sadness and *accedia* which it inspires or accompanies.[116] This singular old man had forgotten these considerations or at least, in his eagerness for tears, he had somewhat overlooked them. 'Father, should a monk ever think of his parents, even if they are dead?' The form of this question would seem to prepare a negative answer, but no: 'The old man replied, "If you know that this remembrance brings compunction to your soul, give yourself to it. When tears come, all you have to do is direct them to the object that you wish, whether your sins or some other appropriate thought."'[117] This craftiness shows at least how desirable *penthos* appeared to Eastern monks.

## VII

## OBSTACLES TO *PENTHOS*

A FTER THE CHAPTER on means must come one on obstacles. The first of these is, of course, neglect of the prescribed exercises: examination of conscience, meditation on the last things, manifestation of conscience. Then come attachment to the goods of this world and the dissipation which results. It is possible, though, to go deeper than this, to underlying inner dispositions. The early Fathers usually speak of these in negative terms, which is hardly surprising, since the word which expresses the immediate goal of all ascesis is itself a negative term, *apatheia*. Saint Jerome would never have waged war against this concept had he realized its true meaning. Despite the etymology which appears to make synonyms of them, the two words 'impassibility' and 'insensitivity' are diametrically opposed. If I may cite here some lines previously written on a different topic:

The terms ἀναισθητός, αναισθητεῖν, ἀναισθησία usually have a pejorative sense. They signify obtuseness, listlessness in spiritual matters, in short the vice of total lukewarmness. This was Origen's understanding,[1] and John Climacus[2] describes it at length in a chapter entitled, 'Insensitivity is the death of the soul before the death of the body'.[3] Evagrius is of the same mind: 'The man who in inner contemplation possesses the spiritual world, ceases from every corruptible desire. He is intensely ashamed of the things he used to do, for

88

his present discernment reproaches him for all his previous insensitivity.'[4] Chapter Two of his *On Evil Thoughts* portrays the horror of this wretched state of mind, but even here he has not dared to say everything. 'Demons oppress the soul when passions are multiplied. They make a man insensitive, paralyzing his spiritual senses, so that he no longer has the slightest feeling for any of the virtuous causes which are his life. If he did have a feeling for them, he would feel himself being drawn from a deep ditch.'[5] 'Both virtues and vices make the intellect blind, the former so that it will not see the vices, the latter so that it will not see the virtues.'[6] To sum it all up in a definition, 'Spiritual sensitivity is impassibility of an intelligent being, a gift of God.'[7] What this says clearly is that spiritual senses quicken to the extent that the lower senses are deadened.[8]

This exposition spares us from dwelling on each of the 'eight evil thoughts', from examining the incompatibility of each one with *penthos*. Of the two greatest foes, sadness and *accedia,* enough has already been said.[9] It may be noticed in passing that the most arid of all the passions, *accedia,* can cause tears as well as any passion, but these are 'the impassioned tears of a childish temperament'.[10] So too with gluttony, for 'dry bread causes tears' in children both old and young.[11] Sooner or later each passion will bring mourning for a lost object and hence (*pace* the old man of the last chapter) it hinders authentic compunction. Another old man puts it nicely:

One day, seeing his disciple weighed down from eating (he had had visitors that afternoon), he took him aside and said, 'Do you not realize that *penthos* is a small lighted lamp? Unless you shelter it carefully, it will go out in an instant and its flame will disappear. Excessive eating puts it

out, as do prolonged sleep, evil speaking, and
gossip. In a word, every relaxation of the flesh
chases it away, makes it disappear.'[12]

It is superfluous to speak of lust; its total monopoly of the
senses causes an equally total dulling of sensitivity to any
helpful influence. Love of money stifles that spirit of poverty
which is known to be indispensable. If the connection with
anger seems less apparent, one has only to recall the nature
of this vice—the tendency to complain of another instead of
oneself. By eliminating self-blame it cuts off *penthos* at its
root. There remain vainglory and pride, and here we must
look more closely.

One could, of course, simply refer to what has already
been said on the necessity of humility. Seen from the
exterior, is there a single human action which cannot be
interpreted as the result of pride? For 'it is difficult to escape
the thought of vainglory. The very thing you do to destroy
it [such as humiliation, repentance, remembrance of sins],
even that becomes for you the basis of new vanity.'[13]

I am amazed at the skill of demons when I see how
they take advantage of every occasion. The sackcloth of repentance will serve them for vainglory
as well as princely raiment, words as well as
silence, satiety as well as hunger, retreat as well as
society. Rightly did one of the brothers call vainglory a thistle which stings on all sides. Let us
remember that Christ was crowned with thorns,
not thistles, thus showing by allegory how hard it
is to reject them.[14]

To examine our thoughts for vainglory or humility is to
end in a vicious circle. I am proud, but I am aware of it,
so that is humility. And vice versa. Humility achieves its goal
only by forgetting itself and thus considering its essence. To
think oneself a sinner and to hold all men as better than
oneself ('A dog is better than I am,' said Abba Xanthias, 'for
he has love and he does not judge'[15] is undoubtedly a sign of

humility and a step toward compunction, but it cannot begin
to define a virtue which was never more fully possessed than
by the spotless Virgin. The early monks made no mistake about
this. Pride consists in forgetting that God is God, and humility
in not forgetting that I am a creature of God. Evagrius'
chapter on pride in the *Antirrheticon* is clearly based on this
idea. Vanity, a lesser form of pride, consists in behaving
toward others as a minor god who can claim their special
admiration, as one who is predestined to command, one who
considers any slight to himself as foolish and unjust. The
essence of pride is, to use the word of Evagrius and Saint
Maximus, φιλαυτία, that is, the hardening of one's will against
the will of God. So speak Saints Barsanuphius, Theodore the
Studite and many others. 'To cut off one's will'—this short
formula sums up for them the whole secret of perfection. To
do this is to cut away the root of all passions and to cause all
the virtues to bloom.[16] Vanity must be opposed by
*apsephiston,* an untranslatable term which contains a wealth
of analysis and experience: not to give oneself, or to claim
from others, the allowance of any privilege or distinction.
To consent therefore to be nothing at all, or better, to hold
this fast (κρατεῖν), to take possession of it (κατέχειν). If we
do not have perpetual compunction, it is because of our
stubbornness, perhaps half-unconscious, against the divine
will, and our unscrupulous campaigning for human vainglory.

Saint Barsanuphius convinces us of this with his accustomed frankness:

> Since I have many sins, a correspondent writes,
> I wish to do penance, but because of the weakness
> of my body I am unable to maintain the asceticism
> of the Fathers. What should I do?
> Reply: If you wish to begin doing penance, think
> of the sinful woman who washed the Lord's feet
> with her tears. Tears cleanse us from our sins. Yet
> they only come with great effort after long applica-
> tion and endurance, through meditation on the

dread judgement and eternal shame, and through
self-denial, according to the Master's word: 'whoever would follow me, let him deny himself, take
up his cross and follow me.' Now to deny oneself
and take up one's cross is to cut off one's will in
everything and to hold to the *apsephiston.*[17]

It all comes to the sacrifice of that 'I' which is our will. This
is always the last stronghold we want to give up, but we have
no other choice.

Excuse me, Father in the Lord. I know that the
Fathers tell us to enter our cell and to remember
our sins. It is useless for me to recall them, because
I experience no sadness. I often desire compunction, but it does not come. Tell me, then, what
prevents it from coming.

*Reply:* Brother, you deceive yourself in saying
that you want this, because you do not really want
it. To go into your cell is an act of your soul, just
like an examination of conscience and recollection
of thoughts, far from any man. When these things
are done we will have sorrow and compunction.
Therefore, what prevents compunction from coming to you is your will. If a man does not cut off
his own will, his heart will not be moved. It is lack
of faith which keeps you from cutting off your
own will, and lack of faith comes from our desire
for human glory. The Lord has said, 'How can you
believe, you who accept glory from men and do
not seek the glory which comes from God alone?'
I may wish to prevent water from reaching your
stomach from your mouth, but you are drawing it
in through your nose. That is the fatal *dikaioma*
[mania for self-justification] which draws a man
into hell. That is why the most savage demons
make sport of you and render easy things difficult.
Instead of asking me questions, leave your will and

your mania for self-justification, or I will leave you. If you will not work at cutting off your will, even when your heart does not wish it, what good are your questions? You give your hundred denarii and I will provide the thousand talents. But see now, when your former sins are pardoned, you scheme to find ways to slip through the little hidden door of self-justification into a still worse state. Cease, brother; this way is not good. Amma Sarah has said, 'If I wished to please all men, I should find myself a penitent at the door of each one.'[18] And the Apostle says, 'If I pleased men, I would not be the slave of Christ.' If you really wish to weep for your sins, be watchful over yourself, and die to the eyes of every man. It is a hard task, brother, to save a man. Cut off these three things: your will, self-justification, and human self-satisfaction. Then compunction will come to you in all truth, and God will shelter you from every evil. Brother, I charge you to be watchful over yourself, rejoicing when you are struck, reproved, insulted, punished. Cast away the serpent's wiles, but not his prudence. Keep the dove's simplicity together with prudence, and the Lord will come to your aid. This is the way of salvation. If you wish, walk in it, and the Lord will hold out his hand to you. If you cannot, that is your business. Each man has freedom for what he wants. If you turn it over to another, you will be without care; it is he who will bear your cares. Choose what you will.[19]

This brusque letter deserved translation.[20] The great elder's asperity, directed against someone who claimed to desire compunction, is a perfect illustration of his view that the great obstacle to compunction lies in one's own will, the essence of vanity and pride.

Certain aspects of vanity require special mention, because the Fathers have spoken of them more often as being more frequent or harmful. First there is *parrhesia*. By its etymology, this word means the right or custom of saying everything. The word has evolved in two directions. There is the positive meaning: confidence and boldness before God, founded on a good conscience.[21] The other is pejorative: excessive liberty of words or manners with other people, the casual behavior of someone aware of his own worth.[22] The first is among the finest charisms;[23] the other is a vice, worse than all others. Saint Dorotheos even claimed that it begets the other vices.[24] Nor is this rhetorical exaggeration: Diadochus of Photice,[25] John Chrysostom,[26] and the Lausiac History[27] say the same thing when they attribute this detestable parentage to οἴησις. The latter differs from *parrhesia* only as the interior cause from the outward symptom of the same spiritual sickness, pride and vanity.

Abba Peter, the disciple of Abba Lot, said, 'One day when I was in Abba Agathon's cell, a brother came in and said to him, "I want to live with the brethren; tell me how to dwell with them." The old man answered him, "All the days of your life keep the stranger's frame of mind which you have on the first day you join them, so as not to become too familiar with them." Abba Macarius asked, "And what does this familiarity produce?" The old man replied, "It is like a strong, burning wind, each time it arises everything flies swept before it, and it destroys the fruit of the trees." So Abba Macarius said, "Is speaking too freely really as bad as all that?" Abba Agathon said, "No passion is worse than an uncontrolled tongue, because it is the mother of all the passions. Accordingly the good workman should not use it, even if he is living as a solitary in the cell. I know a brother who spent a long time in his cell using a small bed who said, "I should have left my cell without making use of that small bed if no-one had told me it was there". It is the hard-working monk who is a warrior.'[28]

The hot wind of *parrhesia* will dry all tears of compunction, as we are told by one who refers to the same saying of Agathon:

Laughter and *parrhesia* spell disaster for the monk's soul. When you find yourself in this state, O monk, know that you have reached the depth of evils. Do not cease to pray that God may withdraw you from this death. Laughter and an uncontrolled tongue cast monks, old as well as young, into shameful passions; they draw the monk downwards. Of *parrhesia* one of the saints said, 'It is like a burning wind which kills the fruits of the monk'. As for laughter, consider this thought: laughter casts out the blessedness of *penthos* and demolishes what had been built. Laughter saddens the Holy Spirit; it does no good to the soul and it corrupts the body. Laughter puts the virtues to flight. It has neither the remembrance of death nor consideration of its punishments. O Lord, remove laughter from me, and give me the *penthos* and the tears which you require from me, O God . . . . [29]

What connection can there be between the vices of *parrhesia* and this laughter which seems so innocent? Simply that the latter is the sign of the former. A man does not laugh if he thinks he has something to fear from his sins and divine justice. 'Do not laugh, brother, or you will chase away the fear of God', said an old man to a young novice,[30] and Theodore the Studite was to repeat the saying without softening it in the least.[31] It is clear that *penthos* and laughter exclude each other; if psychology were not enough to convince us of this, we could always learn it from a contrast drawn by Our Lord.[32] A word, then, must be said about laughter, although the Fathers furnish enough material for a separate article on the subject.

'Is it ever permitted to laugh?' someone asked Saint Basil. What sort of an answer will we hear from the man whom Saint Gregory Nazianzen portrays as so amiable, even playful?[33] Perhaps Gregory is stretching the truth slightly when, in his Panegyric, he presents his friend as the perfect model of that golden mean which he considers the ideal of virtue. Or perhaps Saint Basil did not take his own teaching literally. Here, in any case, are the moralist's words:

> In the Gospel Jesus Christ condemns those who laugh now. It follows that the faithful can find no time to laugh during this life, especially when he considers how many there are who dishonor God through breaking his law and who die in their sins, when he sees the deplorable state to which they are reduced, deserving only groans and tears.[34]

The Long Rules show less absolutism:

> That laughter also must be held in check. Those who live under discipline should avoid very carefully even such intemperate action as is commonly regarded lightly. Indulging in unrestrained and immoderate laughter is a sign of intemperance, of a want of control over one's emotions, and of failure to repress the soul's frivolity by a stern use of reason. It is not unbecoming, however, to give evidence of merriment of soul by a cheerful smile, if only to illustrate that which is written: 'A glad heart maketh a cheerful countenance' (Prov 15: 13); but raucous laughter and uncontrollable shaking of the body are not indicative of a well-regulated soul, of personal dignity, or self mastery.

Scriptural citations follow, all from the Old Testament. One Gospel verse will be given later on, but only a faint allusion to 'Woe to you who laugh'. Saint Basil continues:

Moreover, the Lord appears to have experienced those emotions which are of necessity associated with the body, as well as those that betoken virtue, as, for example, weariness and compassion for the afflicted; but, so far as we know from the story of the Gospel, he never laughed. On the contrary, he even pronounced unhappy those who are given to laughter. And let not the equivocal sense of the word 'laughter' deceive us, for it is a frequent practice in the Scriptures to call joy of spirit and the cheerful feeling which follows upon good actions, 'laughter'. Sarah says, for instance, 'God has made a laughter for me,' (Gen 21:6) and there is another saying, 'Blessed are you who weep now, for you shall laugh' (Lk 6:21).[35]

One may draw one's own conclusions on the difference between these two opinions. If Saint Basil's thought did develop, it was in the more rigorist direction, for the Short Rules are later than the Long Rules.[36] To justify his modest smile, the great bishop cites the Old Testament almost exclusively. Philo Judaeus, despite the pessimism which he inherited from the philosophers and which made him also ask 'whether it is possible for anyone to laugh', nevertheless finds justification in his sacred Book for becoming the apologist for that sign of joy 'which is created by God', even though he reserves this to the wise and perfect.[37] Here the Old Testament is, according to Saint John Chrysostom, less severe than the New:

> Even as it is difficult, or rather impossible, to mix fire and water, so it seems to me that pleasure and compunction are incompatible. One brings forth tears and sobriety, the other laughter and foolishness. One renders the soul light and wingèd, the other makes it heavier than the heaviest lead. The most extraordinary thing is that David (a model of compunction) lived in times which were not very

strict in matters of conduct. We, on the other hand, have joined combat at an hour when not only the other vices, but even laughter incurs great punishments, while *penthos* and affliction are praised on all sides.[38]

Alas! Already in the late fourth century,

Christianity is no longer anything but good manners, politeness. There is nothing stable, nothing weighty and lasting. I speak not only to those in the world; I know well who are the objects of my words. The Church is full of nothing but laughter and mockery. If someone speaks a good word, immediately those who are seated in the holy places burst out laughing and, what is even more amazing, there are some who do not control themselves even at the time of prayer. The devil must be leaping for joy, if I may so speak; he is clothing everyone with his spirit, he is making himself master of the world . . . . Do you not know what Saint Paul says, 'Let no dishonest words be heard among you, nor foolish, nor such as lead to laughter'. You see that he puts buffoonery and dishonesty at the same level . . . . What? You laugh! And where have you heard it said that Jesus Christ laughed? You will not find that anywhere. On the contrary, you will read in several places that he was sad. For he wept, seeing the city of Jerusalem . . . . With all that, you do not cease laughing. He who did not suffer the sins of others deserved to receive their blame, and will he who is unaware of his own sins, and goes so far as to laugh about them, receive pardon?[39]

This is not the place to discuss the authenticity of those writings which Chrysostom's editors classify as spurious. As far as the content is concerned, there is no reason not to accept as genuine the homily entitled, 'That the ascetic should not indulge in mirth'.

It is a terrible thing to dissipate oneself in *eutrapelia*. Laughter looses the bonds of temperance, chases gravity, does not remember the fear of God, does not fear the threat of Gehenna. Laughter is a guide to debauchery, *eutrapelia* is the mark of a dissolute man. Humorous words cause us to lapse into softness, they become the occasion of indifference. That is why the blessed Apostle forbids them: 'Let there be no filthiness, no silly talk, no levity, which are not fitting; but instead let there be thanksgiving' (Eph 5:4). While you laugh, you should fear lest the Lord become angry, he who blesses those who mourn and speaks woe to those who laugh. May the devil not find in your foolishness and shameless laughter a lack of godly fear and forgetfulness of your spiritual interests; may he not take occasion to assault your soul and sow tares. There have been times of greater indulgence for amusement, and yet even then holy men showed great strictness rather than playfulness. So the psalmist: 'All the day I go about mourning' (Ps 38:6), and 'Every night I flood my bed with tears; I drench my couch with my weeping' (Ps 6:7).[40]

The same intransigence is to be found in the Monastic Constitutions attributed to Saint Basil. Chapter twelve opens with the abrupt declaration, 'We must abstain from all laughter'.[41] Saint Thomas Aquinas, on the other hand, counts *eutrapelia* among the virtues. 'Concerning the enjoyments of play there is another virtue which the Philosopher calls *eutrapelia*.'[42] Aquinas read his Saint Paul in Latin and the Eastern ascetics cared little for Aristotle—hence the difference. It is not for me to say whether that difference is real or merely verbal.

If there were any among the early monks who did not

live up to this ideal of gravity, it was not for lack of clarity in exhortations or perfection in examples. The countless writings of that adversary of laughter, Saint Ephrem, circulated in every language, even Arabic.[43] Chrysostom, also widely translated, is wholly in agreement on this point with his compatriot 'of the Syriac tongue'. He pursues laughter in all Christians, but especially among monks and women, without however forbidding a smile of relaxation in the proper times and places.[44] He had ample support. No less a figure than Clement of Alexandria devoted a whole chapter of his *Teacher* to proving that 'we must expel from our republic people who affect risible passions'. Further, 'if we must evict buffoons from our republic, how unfitting would it be for us to take it upon ourselves to cause laughter . . . . We must be gracious, and not provoke laughter, much rather, we must put a muzzle on laughter.' In what follows, Clement returns to his pet theory of moderation and conciliation of extremes:

> In a word, we must not take away from man anything that is natural to him, but impose on him limits and proper times. Just because man is a risible animal does not mean that he has to laugh at everything. The horse is a 'whinniable' animal, but he does not whinny constantly.[45]

The laughter of sensible people is called smiling.

Origen puts *abstinentia risus,* together with fasting, genuflexion and the like, among the 'condiments' of our virtuous acts, the main courses being the interior virtues.[46] Saint Gregory Nazianzen allows the monk 'an affable smile, or rather a faint smile, in temperance holding back from immoderate laughter'.[47] In the course of time this lenience will find a few more isolated spokesmen. The good-natured Saint Dorotheos (if the *Doctrina* XXIV is his[48]) has this delightful saying, 'If you must laugh, let your laughter be without teeth'.[49] It is from this saying, perhaps, that the austere saint Theodore the Studite found the boldness to

allow 'a pleasant and cheerful smile for spiritual refresh-
ment',[50] but this is the only passage I know where he allows
such a free rein to permissiveness. One had to be bold to go
even this far, if one had made the Lives of the Fathers one's
daily food. Those men knew no compromise. Although it is
not said that Saint Arsenius never laughed after his retreat
to the desert, that conclusion is inescapable, and the same is
true for many others. It was considered shameful for a monk
to give in to such weakness. It even appears that, in contrast
to other faults, they did not admit their lapses willingly. Of
course there is Agathon, who did not protest against the
accusation of being a charlatan, having devised a system of
recognizing in himself all defects, save the crime of heresy.[51]
But then there is Pambo, who defended his reputation with
the subtlety of a philologist:

> They said of Abba Pambo that his face never
> smiled. So one day, wanting to make him laugh,
> the demons stuck wing feathers on to a lump of
> wood and brought it in making an uproar and
> saying, 'Go, go'. When he saw them Abba Pambo
> began to laugh and the demons started to say in
> chorus, 'Ha! Ha! Pambo has laughed!' But in reply
> he said to them, 'I have not laughed, but I made
> fun of your powerlessness, because it takes so
> many of you to carry a wing.'[52]

When a cenobite was weary of common observances, Saint
Euthymius told him the well-known story of the angry monk
who had hoped to free himself from his vice by becoming a
hermit, and who fell back into storms of rage because of a
glass of water turned over by 'some unknown trick of the
evil one'.

> At these words Clematius, warming to the wit of
> the story, began to laugh. But the divine Euthy-
> mius, staring at him, said, 'Now brother, have you
> too been tickled by some crafty demon, that you
> are laughing without modesty or shame when you

should be groaning and weeping, expecting the
consolation which must follow? Perhaps you think
that he who must judge us way lying when he
called those who weep blessed, for they will be
comforted, and spoke woe to those who laugh
unguardedly. It is quite improper for a monk to
speak more than is necessary, to give in to his first
impressions, or to indulge in *parrhesia*. For the
Fathers call *parrhesia* the mother of all the passions.' After this scolding, Clematius went into his
inner cell, and retribution followed on his heels.
He fell face down on the ground, shaken with
trembling and seized with fright . . . ' [53]
to the point that his confrères went to intercede for him
with Euthymius. He allowed himself to be moved, and went
to raise up the culprit, recommending that he 'watch over
himself, no longer scorning the teachings and counsels of
the Fathers'.

In spite of this, Euthymius' biographer, Cyril of Scytho-
polis, makes much of his gentleness and friendliness. His
easy-going nature did not, evidently, go so far as to allow
finding humor in the sayings of the Fathers. Karl Heussi may
just be right when he says, 'The more I study the *Apophthegmata*, the clearer it is to me that the element of humor is
rarely found there. Many passages which today seem to us
humorous or ironic most probably had at the time a totally
serious intent.'[54] Nothing could be more pleasant than
Theodoret's *Historia Religiosa,* and yet he warns us in his
prologue that his heroes and heroines 'knew nothing of the
passion of laughter and spent all their life in tears and weeping'.[55] In spite of this, one of his saints appeared one day
bursting with joy. The others were amazed, 'for he always
had an austere look, and now everyone saw him smiling'.
Something dramatically sudden must have happened. In point
of fact, Saint Julian Sabas had just learned through revelation of the death of his namesake, the apostate emperor.[56]

When, then, Theodoret explains that the great inspiration of these wonderful lives was divine Eros, we must conclude that the flame of this love left *penthos* intact while consuming its opposite, laughter.

There are many other shining examples of the same qualities, but we will cite only two more, a man and a woman. In the Life of Saint Abraham Qīdūnaiā, whose feats inspired the poetic verve of Saint Ephrem, we read, 'In the whole course of his life he did not let a single day pass without tears. Laughter never approached his lips, not even a smile.'[57] The biographer is ecstatic: 'Oh marvellous glory! Truly, my brothers, I am amazed at the works of his *ascesis,* at his frequent watches, his tears, his sleeping on the ground.' One can understand Saint Ephrem's enthusiasm for this sort of sanctity. Now here is Saint Marina: 'None of the brothers ever saw her face merry or laughing. She was in mourning all the days of her life.'[58]

The matter is summed up for us by an unknown writer using the name of Ephrem: 'The Fathers of old, who were perfect, observed what they had once begun until death, according to an unchanging rule. For forty or fifty years they made no changes in their customs, that is, in their beautiful and faultless manner of life . . . , with all this, vigils and prayers with tears and compunction, abstinence from laughter and even from smiling . . . . '[59] The meaning of these last words is not certain. Father Zingerle translates, 'at the most a little smile',[60] but it seems more probable that even smiling was forbidden. On the other hand, in the text just cited about Abraham Barkidunaya, the meaning is probably that the saint allowed himself to smile, even though Lamy writes, '*ne subridebat quidem*'. Perhaps the Fathers themselves were not in perfect agreement on the subject of laughter.

Monks were not the only ones for whom these proscriptions were intended. In Egypt, the favorite soil of primitive monasticism, laughter was mentioned at baptism among the

other pomps of Satan, if we are to believe the late thirteenth-
century Coptic theologian, Ibn Saba:

> While [the candidate at baptism] stands to re-
> nounce Satan, he must first abandon pride, hate,
> rancor, calumny, lying, murder, adultery, theft,
> false witness, blasphemy, laughter, mockery, hypo-
> crisy  and all the works of Satan, things which he
> declares he renounces.[61]

Saint Nilus wrote to a layman:

> I praise you for the great care you show for your
> soul, for your abstention from evil spectacles, for
> your patience and for the other virtues which you
> show in your life in the world. There is only one
> more thing which I ask you to do for me: from
> now on keep yourself far from the plague of those
> who cause laughter, and then your crown will be
> complete.[62]

It was to another layman that Saint Theodore the Studite
sent a list of sins to avoid, including, on the same line as
debauchery, laughter.[63] In the seventh century a monk
of Mar Saba, Antiochus, summed up the common doctrine
on this and other points. He gave his Homily Ninety-five
the pithy title περὶ τοῦ μὴ γελᾶν, that is, 'On not laughing'.
This is a far cry from the rendering given by that *traduttore-
traditore,* Fronton du Duc: *'Temperandum a solutiore et
immoderato risu.'* After all, look at the first sentence:
'Christians and above all monks are absolutely forbidden to
laugh.' This prohibition is supported by numerous biblical
and patristic citations. 'And so, beloved, let us use all our
vigilance to avoid being caught by the enemy in the nets of
laughter, for numerous are the embarrassments and the
diabolical passions which it breeds. Laughter is for stupid
people, or rather for the imbeciles who make a profession of
pandering to the world on their stage.' The chapter, dread-
fully emasculated by Fronton du Duc, ends as it should in the
spirit of the Gospel beatitude: 'Blessed are those who have

*penthos,* for they will be comforted.'[64]

All such rigorism, then, can be explained by the desire for perpetual compunction. Saint Anthony's disciple, Saint Ammonas, gives us the final word:

> Be sure to ask truthfully for pardon of your sins. Seek the salvation of your soul and the kingdom of heaven in every way possible. Try with all your strength to humble yourself in thoughts, words, works, through your dress and deportment. Make yourself lower than dung, dust, and ashes, as the last of all and the servant of all. Consider yourself always, from the depth of your heart and in truth, as the last and most sinful of Christians, far removed from every virtue. Say to yourself, 'In comparison with other Christians I am only dust and ashes, and like a polluted garment (Is 64:6), and it is only through great favor and grace that I can find mercy before God, since I deserve eternal punishment more than life. For, if he wishes to enter into judgement with me I cannot find vindication, since I am totally abject.' Keep your soul in mourning and humiliation, therefore, and expect death each day. Cry ceaselessly to God so that with great mercy he may correct your soul and have pity on you, so that you may feel yourself overcome with mourning and groans. Then instead of merriment and laughter, your laugh will be changed to *penthos* and your joy into compunction, and you will always walk with a sombre air, saying, 'I groan because of the tumult of my heart' (Ps 38:8).[65]

Other liberties that one may take, for instance with detachment from material goods, can be no less fatal to *penthos.* We have seen that a knife hung from a belt can dry the source of tears.[66] It does not require even that much: 'An old man said, "Clearly, if a man is a warrior, God requires that he have no attachment to any material object, even a little needle, for this could prevent his thought from conversation with Jesus and from compunction".'[67]

Among the obstacles to compunction, we must unfortunately mention certain liturgies. The time came when psalmody threatened to be trodden underfoot by compositions inspired more by the muses than the Holy Spirit. What is the earliest date of the compositions we are about to hear of? Certainly not the fourth century, despite the appearance of Abba Pambo's name. In our ignorance we can only recommend that historians of liturgy do the necessary research. We know that in the eleventh century Paul Evergetinos cited the following passage to remind his contemporaries of older liturgical spirituality—a proof that the text still said something to the men of that time.

> Abba Pambo had sent his disciple to Alexandria to sell the produce of his work. There he spent, as he told us, sixteen days. At night he slept in the narthex of the church, at the sanctuary of the holy apostle Mark. After seeing the office at that church, he returned to the old man; he had even learned the *troparia*. The old man said to him, 'I see that you are troubled, my child. Did any temptation come to you in the city?' The brother replied, 'Oh, abba, we waste our days in this desert in listlessness, without singing canons or *troparia*. During my stay in Alexandria I saw the clerics of the church. How they sing! This makes me sad. Why do we not also sing canons and *troparia*?' The old man said to him, 'Woe to us, my child. The time is coming when monks will abandon solid food, as the Holy Spirit says, to give themselves to odes and tones (ἄσμασι καὶ ἤχοις). What sort of compunction or tears do you think can arise from these *troparia* when one stands in church or in one's cell, raising one's voice like an ox? If

indeed it is before God that we stand, we must
hold ourselves in his presence with much compunction, not with fine airs. Monks did not come into
this solitude to strut around before God, singing
canticles, scanning melodies, waving their hands
and jumping from one foot to the other. We should
rather, in the fear of God and in trembling, in tears
and groans, with a voice full of reverence and
prompt to compunction, contained and humble,
offer our prayers to God. I warn you, my child, the
time will come when Christians will corrupt the
books of the holy apostles and the divine prophets,
when they will scratch out the holy Scriptures to
write *troparia* and hellenic discourses. They will
swoon over the new and disdain the old. That is
why our fathers told us that dwellers in the desert
should not write the lives and discourses of the
Fathers on parchment, but on papyrus, because the
generation to come is getting ready to scratch out
the lives of the Fathers and to write in whatever
their fancy dictates. Great is the calamity which
is coming' . . . .

There follows a terrifying exposé of the state to which
Christianity will then be reduced:

Superiors will scorn their own salvation and that of
their own flock. They will all be fervent and
observant at meals. They will be quick to quarrel
but slow to pray, ready to speak ill of others and
pass judgement, without wishing to imitate or even
hear the lives and discourses of the old men.
Instead they will revile them, saying, 'If we had
lived in their time, we would have fought as good a
fight as they . . . ' . In the time to come, he who
will save his soul will save it, and he will be called
great in the kingdom of heaven.

Abba Silvanus is of the same opinion:

A brother asked him, 'What shall I do, Abba? How shall I obtain compunction? I am very much tormented by accedia, by sleep and drowsiness. When I get up after sleep, I make a real effort with psalmody, but I cannot shake off my torpor. I cannot even say a psalm without accompanying it with an air.' The old man answered him, 'My child, to say psalms with melodies is first of all pride, for that suggests to you the thought that you are singing, whereas your brother is not singing. Secondly, this hardens your heart and prevents you from entering into compunction. If then you desire compunction, drop your chanting. When you are standing for your prayers, let your spirit dwell on the sense of the verse. Reflect that you are in the presence of God who tests the reins and the heart. The minute you get up from sleep, let your mouth praise God, then recite the symbol of faith and the Our Father. Then begin your office deliberately, groaning and meditating on your sins and the punishment to which they are subject.' The brother said, 'Ever since I became a monk, Abba, I have sung the sequence of the office according to the office-book.' The old man replied, 'And that is precisely why *catanyxis* and *penthos* have escaped you. Think of the illustrious Fathers, how simple they were. They knew neither modes nor *troparia,* but only a few psalms, and yet they shone as luminaries in the universe. Such were Abba Paul the Simple, Abba Pambo, Abba Apollo and the other God-fearing Fathers. They did great marvels, they even raised the dead, and they received their power against demons not in odes, *troparia* and varied tones, but in a prayer full of compunction and in fasting. These are the things which bring to the heart a perpetual fear of God; by them

*penthos* is strengthened, purifying a man of all sin
and rendering the spirit whiter than snow. As for
song, it has brought many to the depths of the
earth, and not only people of the world. Even
priests have by this means become effeminate and
have fallen into lewdness and other shameful passions. Thus chant is for the worldly, for where the
people gather in churches. Think, my child, how
many hierarchies there are in heaven, and of none
of them is it written that it sings according to the
office-book. Rather, one order ceaselessly says
*Alleluia,* another *Holy, holy, holy is the Lord God
of Hosts,* and another *Blessed be the glory of the
Lord in his holy place and in his dwelling.* As for
you, my child, imitate the Fathers if you wish in
your prayers to acquire compunction by keeping,
as far as you can, your spirit from every distraction. Love Christ's humility. Wherever you go, do
not set yourself up as a keen mind or as a professor, but as a simple person, as a student. Then
God will grant you compunction.'[68]

These last words lead us to a new obstacle to compunction. It is an occupation, one which professors of theology
would not expect to see mentioned here and yet it must be
mentioned, in faithfulness to the Fathers. After all, the
literature also contains sources of encouragement for those
who are intellectuals by duty and who lack the gift of tears.
Just as 'the lives and sayings of the old men enlighten the
soul, filling it with spiritual tears', so 'discourses on the faith
and the reading of dogmatic books dry up a man's compunction'.[69] There are two reasons for forbidding theological discussions: fear of heresy, and humility. Heussi has
dealt with the first of these, Reitzenstein with the second.[70]
It must be added that both reasons fuse into one, because
theology is reserved for those who are perfect. A letter of
Saint Barsanuphius makes this point:

Is it good always to tell fine stories drawn from Scripture and the lives of the Fathers?

*Reply:* Everyone knows that honey is sweet. It is also known that the author of Proverbs says, 'If you have found honey, eat only enough for yourself, lest you be sated with it and vomit it' (Prov 25:16). There are many kinds of sacks. Some contain one measure, others contain three. If you try to force the smaller sack to hold three measures, it will not take them. It is the same here; we cannot consider all men as equals. One can speak without harm, the other cannot. Great and admirable, therefore, above all things is silence. It is this which the Fathers esteemed and embraced, it is by this that they became glorious . . . . But since we, through our weakness, cannot walk in the way of the perfect, let us speak what tends to edification, finding it in the words of the Fathers, not risking the stories of Scripture. The latter is dangerous for the uninstructed, because they were said spiritually, and the unspiritual man cannot understand spiritual things. In fact it is written, 'The letter kills, but the spirit gives life' (2 Cor 3:6). Let us then take refuge in the words of the Fathers, and we will find there the profit which belongs to them.[71]

This profit consists in reminding ourselves that we do not practice what we read and speak.

This feeling of incapacity reaches far back in time. Evagrius said nothing new when he wrote, 'He who has not seen God cannot talk of him'.[72] He is doing nothing more than transposing a common monastic theme into his philosophical system. It was so common that one must often read it between the lines in order to grasp the reasoning of the early spiritual writers.

Once Dosithy came to Saint Dorotheos and asked him about a word of Holy Scripture. He was just beginning, because of his purity, to understand some passages of Scripture. As for Dorotheos, he had so far preferred that Dosithy not so apply himself, but rather that he abstain from it through humility. To his questioning he therefore replied, 'I do not know'. Dosithy, attaching no importance to this reply, came back again and asked him about another chapter. So Dorotheos said to him, 'I do not know, but go and ask the Abbot'. He went, suspecting nothing. Now the blessed man had already gone secretly to the Abbot and said, 'If Dosithy comes to ask you about some text of Scripture, rebuke him a little'. When then he came and put his question, the Abbot began to rebuke him and said, 'Will you be still, you who know nothing? You have the boldness to ask such questions! Why don't you think about your impurity?' And he sent him away with other similar words, even giving him two slaps. As for him, he went back to Abba Dorotheos and, showing him his cheeks still red from the blows, he said, 'I got it, solidly!'[73]

Nothing more explicit had to be said to readers who knew the sayings of the Fathers by heart. A famous anchorite had heard such great things of Saint Poemen that he undertook a long voyage to enjoy the profit of his conversation.

Abba Poemen received him with joy. They greeted one another and sat down. The visitor began to speak of the Scriptures, of spiritual and of heavenly things. But Abba Poemen turned his face away and answered nothing. Seeing that he did not speak to him, the other went away deeply grieved and said to the brother who had brought him, 'I have made this long journey in vain. For I have come to see the old man, and he does not wish to speak to me.' Then the brother went inside to

Abba Poemen and said to him, 'Abba, this great
man who has so great a reputation in his own
country has come here because of you. Why did
you not speak to him?' The old man said, 'He is
great and speaks of heavenly things and I am lowly
and speak of earthly things. If he had spoken of
the passions of the soul, I should have replied, but
he speaks to me of spiritual things and I know
nothing about that.' Then the brother came out
and said to the visitor, 'The old man does not
readily speak of the Scriptures, but if anyone con-
sults him about the passions of the soul, he replies.'
Filled with compunction, the visitor returned to
the old man and said to him, 'What should I do,
Abba, for the passions of the soul master me?' The
old man turned towards him and replied joyfully,
'This time, you come as you should. Now open
your mouth concerning this and I will fill it with
good things'. Greatly edified, the other said to him,
'Truly, this is the right way!' He returned to his
own country giving thanks to God that he had
been counted worthy to meet so great a saint.[74]

Such is the true way. Remember that this is the same
Poemen who said, 'Weeping is the way the Scriptures and
our Fathers give us . . . . Truly there is no other way than
this.'[75] Echoes of contemporary controversies rarely troubled
the peace of the desert; if the wind brought them, ears were
stopped. A great dispute arose among the learned whether
Melchizedek is the son of God or a man like the patriarchs.
These were the days of Saint Cyril of Alexandria, so the
solitaries of lower Egypt referred the matter to the archbishop.[76] If there were no bishop at hand, should not the
question still be resolved?

One day the inhabitants of Scetis assembled
together to discuss Melchizedek and they forgot
to invite Abba Copres. Later on they called him

and asked him about this matter. Tapping his mouth three times, he said, 'Alas for you, Copres! For that which God commanded you to do, you have put aside, and you are wanting to learn something which you have not been required to know about.' When they heard these words, the brothers fled to their cells.[77]

Copres would have pleased Saint Anthony:

One day some old men came to see Abba Anthony. In the midst of them was Abba Joseph. Wanting to test them, the old man suggested a text from the Scriptures, and, beginning with the youngest, he asked them what it meant. Each gave his opinion as he was able. But to each one the old man said, 'You have not understood it'. Last of all he said to Abba Joseph, 'How would you explain this saying?' and he replied, 'I do not know'. Then Abba Anthony said, 'Indeed, Abba Joseph has found the way, for he has said, "I do not know".'[78]

There is a very simple way to find the connection between this attitude and compunction. Just think of the necessity of thinking ill of oneself, of blaming oneself. Who would dare trespass into a theology reserved for those so far from the flesh, so advanced in the spirit? It would require, more than boldness, the blindness of those who forget they are sinners. Philoxenus of Mabboug, bishop that he was, understood this difficulty:

Only he who has come to this degree [of perfection] ought to treat of questions touching divinity. I, who have not taken even the first steps in this way, have been asked by you to speak of what lies at the journey's end, of the heavenly Jerusalem, of all its treasures, and of the King who dwells there. Grace can, to be sure, lead the intellect by any way it wishes and bring it, not by the way of *ascesis* but by the path of faith, to the vision of

truth. We will therefore speak through faith of the
gifts received by grace. We will discourse, not in
virtue of the knowledge which can only come from
spiritual love, but only by the instinct of that faith
which is the beginning of the ascetic way of life.[79]

Dogmatic theologians may find this distinction reassuring.
The ascetics, though, may well have thought that one falls
back from faith to a knowledge which is 'simple', 'pragma-
tic', and, worst of all, profane. 'Cranes fly in the form of a
letter, but do not know the alphabet,' remarks the wise
Evagrius.[80]

Poor Evagrius! Still a true disciple of the Fathers when he
spoke of compunction, he never suspected that one day he
himself would be singled out by an authentic heir of the
tradition as an object lesson for teaching the incompatibility
of _penthos_ and theological speculation. The writing in
question was, admittedly, a hazardous one. 'A brother
consulted the holy old man Barsanuphius: "I do not know
how it is, Father, but I have come upon the books of Origen
and Didymus, the _Gnostica_ of Evagrius and the writings of
his disciples".' There follows a summary of their doctrine.
Then:

> _Reply:_ Brother, woe and calamity has come to our
> race! What have we abandoned, and for what are
> we curious? With what are we busy, and towards
> what are we blind? We have left the straight paths
> and we wish to walk in winding ones, so that the
> word of Scripture may be fulfilled concerning us:
> Woe to those who leave the straight ways to walk
> in winding paths! I say this in all truth, brother.
> I have put aside mourning for myself, and I take it
> up for you, seeing where you have fallen. I have for-
> gotten to weep for my sins, and I weep over you as
> over my own child. The heavens shudder when they
> see what men are involved in . . . . Brothers, here
> below is work and in heaven the wages; here the

struggle, there the crown. Brother, if you wish to
be saved, do not throw yourself into these things!
. . . . From now on then abstain from these things,
and walk in the Father's footsteps. Obtain humility, obedience, tears, *ascesis,* detachment from
possessions, *apsephiston.* Now all such things can
be found in the words of the Fathers and in their
lives. Bring forth fruit worthy of repentance. Do
not look at me who say and do not do, but pray
that I also may arrive at knowledge of the truth, at
the glory of the Holy Trinity.[81]

If it is a demon who incites men to these intellectual
curiosities, he must be devilishly persevering. Not to be done
in, he aroused in his victim the hope of finding more leniency
in the 'other elder', John the Prophet. With a few words John
only supported the verdict of the Great Recluse. The
questioner risked one more assault, and this time John,
weary of battle, allowed him to read in Evagrius 'what is
useful to the soul'.[82] But Barsanuphius had the gift of knowing men's hearts, and his correspondent was 'stupefied and
cast down' to receive several days later the following note:

You have said, or at least thought, 'Why do some
of the fathers now receive the *Gnostica* of Evagrius?' Yes, certain brothers receive these books,
thinking themselves gnostics without asking God if
they are true ones. God, then, has abandoned them
in this matter to their own minds. Be that as it
may, it is neither for me nor for you to give ourselves to these problems. Our time is for examination of our passions, tears and *penthos.*[83]

So much for Evagrius, our scholar then says to himself, but
what of Gregory the Theologian? To give more weight to his
new objections, he allies himself with other brothers.
Barsanuphius is not impressed.

Blessed be the God and Father of our Lord Jesus
Christ, who has blessed us in Christ with every

spiritual blessing in the heavenly places. Amen
(Eph 1:3). Brothers, this is the time to say with
the Apostle, 'I have been a fool! You forced me to
it' (2 Cor 12:11). For you force me to scrutinize
things which are beyond me, and to speak what is
of no profit to the soul, if indeed it is not harmful.
We have abandoned the Apostle Paul who said,
'Let all bitterness and wrath and anger and clamor
and slander be put away from you, with all
malice' (Eph 4:31). And, I would add, all gluttony, all fornication, all avarice, and the other
passions. On their account we must have *penthos*
night and day, weeping ceaselessly so that the
abundance of tears may wash away all their filth.
Impure that we are, may we become pure, just
men from sinners, living men from corpses. Let us
concern ourselves with the account we will have to
render, even for a single word. For it is written:
you will render to each one according to his works,
and again, each of us will have to appear before
the tribunal of Christ to receive the measure of his
deeds, whether good or bad. This is where our
efforts should be directed, as were those of our
Fathers, Abba Poemen and his successors. This
concern will prevent us from self-conceit, from
comparing ourselves with others, and will bring us
to consider ourselves as dust and ashes. The other
concern, on the contrary, inspires us to think ourselves gnostics, pushes us to presumption and con-
ceit, to invidious comparisons in everything, and
withdraws us from humility. Excuse me, brothers,
are you so unoccupied that you have come to this?
If so, come down to the square and wait for the
Master to come and send you into his vineyard. If
the thought of this meeting were to linger in your
heart, you would have no thought for this

foolishness. The prophet forgot to eat his bread, but we are self-indulgent and give ourselves to indifference. It is these faults which cause us to fall into those others. It is not studies which God asks of us, but sanctification, purification, silence, humility . . . . [84]

The next letter recommends that the solutions to scriptural problems be left to those saints to whom God does not fail to entrust these matters, in accord with the needs of every age.[85]

The devil of intellectualism continued to vex the poor monk.

Excuse me, charitable Father, for the Lord's sake. I am very troubled, because I have read a dogmatic book, and I see my heart in turmoil. I am afraid to admit this to you, yet I cannot keep silent because of my thoughts. Therefore, what you command I will do.

*Reply:* Since the devil wishes to thrust you into useless reflections, say what is worrying you. And may God give him no entrance.

This time it is a question of the resurrection of the body. Tell me if the saints will rise in the body that we have now, with bones and nerves, or in a body that is ethereal and smooth?

There follow texts invoked by the partisans of the latter theory.

Now please sort all this out for me, for the love of the Lord, to prevent the enemy from leading me astray, lest I fall through ignorance into his wicked traps. I am shaken on all sides because of my foolishness. I should have kept to your holy words and from the start I should have forbidden myself to seek into things which bring great peril to the soul. Pray for me, Father, that I may get hold of myself and labor in weeping for my sins . . . .

These moving tones succeed in softening the rigid elder. For
once he consents to deal with a scholastic problem, but even
here he places his opinion between two significant sayings,
and is clearly more interested in the frame than the picture.

> Brother, I have already written to you that it is
> the devil who has sown in you this inappropriate
> intellectual preoccupation. It is now the season
> for you to weep and to carry *penthos* for your sins.

And at the end:

> Now at last leave this nonsense (μωρολογίας), and
> do not follow the demons and their teachings.
> With one blow they raise you up, and with another
> they cast you down. Humble yourself therefore
> before God, weeping for your sins and in mourn-
> ing for your passions. Remember that Scripture has
> said, 'And now, O Israel', and again, 'Now I begin'.
> From now on be attentive to yourself. May God
> pardon you. You see how your heart is leaning as
> a result of these subtleties.'[86]

Are there no theological questions which are of primary
interest to the spiritual life? Yes, but they must not surpass
all understanding. In what, for example, consist the 'image
and likeness' of God in us? The Fathers themselves had
widely differing ideas about this. Abba Sopatros drew from it
all a practical conclusion for his monks: 'Do not read
apocryphal literature. Do not get involved in discussions
about the image. Although this is not heresy, there is too
much ignorance and liking for dispute between the two
parties in this matter. It is impossible for a creature to understand the truth of it.'[87]

Compunction springs up from two sources: humility and
meditation on the last things. Both of these will be dried up
if we are preoccupied with absorbing and vain curiosities.

Only passing mention need be made of a last obstacle
since it should, at least normally, disappear with age. Young
people, being frivolous and restless, have difficulty with

compunction and might easily disturb the recollection of a
community. Hermits did not want them, and some cenobites
maintained the same restriction. Saint Pachomius was an
innovator in this matter by taking measures to prevent his
monks, including the superior, 'to laugh among children',
and to play with them.[88] Pachomius, though, was no fool.
He hardly expected to see the gift of spiritual tears in adole-
scents. Hence his astonishment when one day he saw the
young Theodore coming toward him 'weeping with heavy
tears. He had not yet been six months with the brothers.[89]
Our father Pachomius said to him, "Why do you weep?" He
was astonished, because he had already seen him many times
in this disposition of tears, and yet he was a young man.'[90]
What in fact was making Theodore weep was the uncertainty
of his salvation. His precociousness dated even farther back.
When still in his father's house, which was 'great in the
world's eyes and prosperous in worldly goods,' on a feast
day, the tenth of December (for such an event deserved exact
dating), he had had 'his heart touched by a divine sentiment
of compunction. And he had reasoned thus within himself:
"If you enjoy these dishes, you will find neither eternal
goods nor true life." Then he withdrew in groans to a peaceful corner of the house. There, falling on his face, he began
to weep and say, "O God, I do not wish the things of this
world; all I want is you and your mercy".'[91]

It has been said before that compunction requires a manly
soul, yet here again, a man's worth is not measured by the
number of his years nor does it necessarily increase with
them. What is needed is the vigor of spiritual maturity. To
borrow the words of Saint Gregory of Nyssa:

> Natural love cannot be kindled in those who are
> still children (for childhood is not susceptible
> to this passion), nor is it seen in those who are
> overwhelmed with extreme old age. So too, when
> it is a matter of divine beauty, neither the child still
> shaken and carried off by every wind of doctrine

nor the old man close to his demise can be reached
by the feelings of this desire. Invisible beauty does
not touch them, but comes only to a soul which
has emerged from infancy and is in the flower of
spiritual age, but which has not yet contracted
spot or wrinkle or anything else of the sort. Only
the soul which has neither the heedlessness of
youth nor the weakness of old age, the soul which
the Canticle calls 'young man', will be amenable to
the first and great command of the Law. With all
his heart and strength he will love that beauty for
which human intelligence can find neither image
nor comparison nor any explanation.[92]

Although the 'old men' use a different vocabulary, their
simplicity is in full accord with the more scholarly language
of Saint Gregory of Nyssa. It is appropriate to end here with
the thought of the love of God. All the virtue which must be
cultivated to produce or conserve *penthos*—concern for
salvation, sorrow for sin, humility, detachment, obedience
and the rest—what are they but forms of that authentic
charity which avoids deceptive words in order better to prove
itself with works? Theodoret was right: it is the passion for
God which gives birth to tears.[93] Yet the passion for God,
according to the unanimous teaching of Eastern spirituality,
can only become total through total victory over the
earthly passions.

VIII

## THE EFFECTS OF *PENTHOS:* PURIFICATION

T HE IDEA OF ONE'S DUTY does not always work as
effectively on the soul as that of one's advantage.
For those with clear vision, of course, the two coin-
cide, but this can only be seen by raising the mind to God,
to his justice and love of man. The Eastern Church knows
that God can command only what is for our good and in
accord with our true nature. We can find a magnificent exposition of this doctrine as early as Saint Irenaeus.[1] Too
often, though, our nearsightedness prevents us from looking
that high and sometimes, in our lack of faith, we fail to be
persuaded by what we know to be true. It will be helpful
then to turn to the effects of 'mourning'. One of these,
although invisible, is well established in Scripture and tradition, while the others are psychologically observable.

In their studied terseness, the sayings of the Fathers
usually omit any mention of a result, or else they say it
in three syllables: 'Do this and *you are saved'.* (καὶ σῴζῃ)
No prospect can equal the attractiveness of that. Salvation is
both eternal happiness and, in this life, the paradise of peace
through the health of the soul. In this context, how often
have we already seen *penthos* recommended as the surest and
indeed the only way. Sometimes the Fathers cause the effects
of *penthos* to shine in the eyes of their questioners without
being very precise as to what they are. Vague promises,
coming from men worthy of confidence, are enticing in their
air of mystery with hope of a beautiful surprise.

A brother said to Abba Peter, the disciple of

121

Abba Lot, 'When I am in my cell, my soul is at peace, but if a brother comes to see me and speaks to me of external things, my soul is disturbed'. Abba Peter told him that Abba Lot used to say, 'Your key opens my door'. The brother said to him, 'What does that mean?' The old man said, 'When someone comes to see you, you say to him, "How are you? Where have you come from? How are the brethren? Did they welcome you or not?" Then you have opened the brother's door and you will hear a great deal that you would rather not have heard.' The brother said to him, 'That is so. What should a man do, then, when a brother comes to see him?' The old man said, 'Compunction is absolute master. One cannot protect oneself where there is no compunction.' The brother said, 'When I am in my cell, compunction is with me, but if someone comes to see me or I go out of my cell, I do not have it any more.' The old man said, 'That means you do not really have compunction at all yet. It is merely that you practice it sometimes. It is written in the Law, "When you buy a Hebrew slave, he shall serve six years and in the seventh he shall go free, for nothing. If you give him a wife and she brings forth sons in your house and he does not wish to go because of his wife and children, you shall lead him to the door of the house and you shall pierce his ear with an awl and he shall become your slave forever" ' (Ex 21:2-6). The brother said, 'What does that mean?' The old man said, 'If a man works as hard as he can at anything, at the moment when he seeks what he needs, he will find it'. The brother said, 'Please explain this to me'. The old man said, 'The bastard will not remain in anyone's service; it is the legitimate son who will not leave his father'.[2]

This brother must have gone away somewhat puzzled. He at least understood that these enigmas were directed at praise, although of a somewhat esoteric variety, of perpetual *penthos*. Other sayings appear equally obscure to us, but they were probably clearer to those who were familiar with the commonplaces of ascetic language. 'Abba Poemen said, "Compunction has two sides: it is a good work and a good protection".'[3] Evagrius puts us on the right track for solving the riddle of these two words: 'What you have been destined for from the beginning is to work and to keep.'[4] This is an allusion to Genesis 2:15, where Adam's job was to till and keep . . . paradise. In this new paradise, we find once again closeness to God:

> An old man said, 'The man who is seated in his cell and who recites psalms is like one who stands outside and seeks the king. But he who prays with tears is like one who holds the king's feet and asks his mercy, just like the courtesan who in a short time washed away all her sins with her tears.'[5]

These last words express the invisible result of compunction. Our authors insist on it to such an extent that one sometimes suspects them of putting comparatively less emphasis on the sacrament of penance. This, it cannot be denied, poses an historical question. At no time in the countless texts which have been cited or could have been cited is *penthos* ever connected with this sacrament. Nor, for that matter, is the efficacity of compunction ever explained by referring to the perfect charity which it brings or should bring. These are problems which I must leave to those with qualifications other than my own.

An expression of Saint Gregory Nazianzen was often to be repeated after him: tears are the fifth baptism. The other four are these: first that of Moses, only in water and so purely allegorical; then that of Saint John the Baptist, greater than the preceding, because a baptism of repentance, but still imperfect because not yet the third, which is baptism in the

Spirit. This is still followed by the baptism in blood, martyrdom, which is the most perfect of all because Christ himself
received it, and because after receiving it there is no further
possibility of stain. Finally there is that of tears, more painful
than martyrdom because it consists in 'nightly bathing one's
bed and covers with tears, . . . taking on the appearance of
mourning and sadness, in imitation of Manasseh and the
Ninevites'.[6] In the following sermon, *On holy baptism,*
Saint Gregory mentions *exagoreusis.* Even if we are to take
this term as meaning sacramental confession, this sacrament
still does nothing to diminish the painful character of the
fifth baptism.

> What a quantity of tears will we produce to equal
> the baptismal fonts? And who is to guarantee us
> that the end of our life will bring us to complete
> health? Who is to say that we will not be handed
> over to the tribunal, still charged with debts and
> required to suffer the fire that lies beyond?
> Doubtless you, O good and charitable Husband-
> man, will pray the Master to spare yet again the fig
> tree, not yet to cut it down, despite the burden of
> sterility which weighs upon it; to allow you once
> again to surround it with dung, that is with tears,
> with groans, with appeals, with sleeping on the
> ground, with vigils, with maceration of the soul
> and body, correcting us with confession and a
> humbler way of life. Yet it is still uncertain
> whether the Master will spare it, since it does no
> good in the place where it is.[7]

From what does the efficacy of the fifth baptism derive—
absolution or washing by tears? Perhaps from both. Yet one
of these cannot replace or alleviate the other. We will soon
see how shallower minds than the 'Theologian's' understood
this doctrine. First let us recall some testimonies which are
independent of Saint Gregory. The Letter of Bishop Ammon
relates how one day, before an assembly of three hundred

monks, Theodore, who was not a priest, made the following remarks:

> It is a long time since God revealed to me what I am going to say to you, enjoining me to be silent until now. But just now while I was standing before him, he ordered me to speak. The message is this: Many of those who have sinned after holy baptism, in almost every place where the name of Christ is preached, and who keep the apostolic faith which we ourselves keep, have wept over their faults. The Lord, accepting the sincerity of their repentance, has erased their sins. All you therefore who up to this day have faithfully wept for your faults committed after baptismal ablution, know that you have received pardon for them. So let each of you give thanks to the Lord's mercy and say, 'You have turned for me my mourning into dancing; you have loosed my sackcloth and girded me with gladness' (Ps 30:11).[8]

Scarcely had this general amnesty been promulgated than the crowning reassurance came in the form of a letter from Saint Anthony. It repeats almost word for word, on the strength of a revelation made to Anthony, the announcement of universal pardon given 'for all sins committed up to the day when you receive this letter, because God has accepted the tears and mourning of those who have wept and borne mourning'.

The repentance of the men of Nineveh inspired many preachers. When Saint Ephrem spoke of it he felt himself transported with enthusiasm.

> The touching tears of these children caused all around them to weep. The little ones' voices penetrated hearts and moved them. Old men covered themselves with ashes, while old women tore out their hair and cast it away. Venerable whitened heads wrapped themselves in pain and

shame. Young people, on seeing their elders, redoubled their groans. Old men provoked the young, those staffs of their old age, to tears.[9]

And so on for many long folio pages. Yet the longer and harder the mourning, the more exuberant will the sinners' joy appear later when Jonah will announce to them, although somewhat reluctantly, God's pardon. The Syrian poet enjoys describing the struggle between the goodness of the Holy Spirit and the harshness of his prophet. A man with no heart, or simply with a bad temper, can resist tears, but never a father; his severity comes from his love. To explain to their children the ways of God, their parents tell them this:

Dear children, how many times have we already punished you? You have endured the whip, and by its blows you have become wiser. It is not through anger that we lifted the rod over you. We were punishing you because you had erred, and we rejoiced to see you corrected by this means. You yourselves understood that the punishment came solely from our love. The whip has done you a service; thanks to it you have become our worthy inheritors. The pain of blows has been filled with joy; the suffering of the rod has been turned into a treasure of delights. Your mourning has changed into pleasure.[10]

No-one is so much a father as God . . . .

Like Saint Gregory, however, Saint Ephrem requires floods of tears. Another great proponent of compunction, Saint John Chrysostom, seems above all to fear the sinner's despair. 'Only do not despair', (μόνον μὴ ἀπογνῷς) is the last word of his message *Ad Theodorum Lapsum*.[11] To prevent discouragement, as well as any excuses, he tried in his homilies *On penitence* to show the easiness of forgiveness. Indeed, we have various ways of obtaining it. 'You are a sinner? Do not despair, but enter the church and manifest your repentance.

You have sinned? Say to God, "I have sinned". What trouble is that? ...' [12]

    You have yet another way of penance. Which one? Mourning for your sins. You have sinned? Be in mourning (πένθησον) and you will cause sin to disappear. What trouble is that? I do not ask more than that you weep (πενθῆσαι) for your sins. I am not telling you to plough the seas, put into ports, set off on an endless journey, spend your wealth, confront savage fleets. But what then? To weep for your sins. 'And where,' you will ask, 'do you get the assurance that in weeping I will destroy sin?' You have the proof of it in Scripture, 'through the example of Manasseh and the Ninevites'. Do you see now that *penthos* erases sins? [13]

In the next homily and still elsewhere Chrysostom comes back to the same ideas with greater emphasis.

    Echoes of this may be found in a curious Greek text entitled *From Saint Anthony and Saint John, on the different ways of finding salvation, and on repentance.* [14] The author lists six ways of obtaining remission for sins. One of these is tears. 'It is still possible to be purified and obtain pardon through a few small tears (δι' ὀλίγων δακρύων), on condition that we in no way persist in our sin. This is how both Peter and the sinful woman were purified and justified. Divine tears are a baptism because they are produced by the Holy Spirit in those who possess them.' This summary recalls both Gregory Nazianzen and John Chrysostom; the compiler merely adds a theological argument of his own. Nonetheless, he also modifies drastically the demands of the Theologian— a few small tears instead of an amount equal to the pool in the baptistery! We should not be too quick to accuse this unknown writer of laxity; he has merely put in the plural an expression used by Chrysostom in the singular:

    The fire of sin is intense. It is put out by a small [amount of] tears (ὀλίγῳ δακρύῳ), for the tear puts out a furnace of faults, and cleans our wounds of sin. David testifies to this and shows the power of tears when he says, 'Every night I wash my bed with tears, I drench my couch with weeping'. Had he wished to insist on the abundance of tears, it would have been enough to say, 'I drench my couch with weeping'. Why then did he add this word, 'I wash?' To show that tears are a bath and a cleansing of faults.[15]

Despite this variance there is a basic unity of teaching concerning the efficacity of *penthos*. Chrysostom is far from contradicting himself when he insists on perpetual compunction while elsewhere affirming the promptness of remission. He himself will tell us how all is reconciled:

Once purified from our faults, we must yet have the same faults before our eyes. God, in his love for men, pardons your sin, but you, for the safety of your soul, keep your sin before your eyes. The remembrance of the past becomes a safeguard for the future. Whoever has remorse for his former acts shows himself more prudent for the future. That is why David says, 'My sin is ever before me'. Having before his eyes his past mistakes, he will not fall into others in the future. That you may know that God requires the same attitude of us, hear the One who says, 'I, I am he who blots out your transgressions, I will remember them no more . . . . Put me in remembrance, let us argue together. Speak first your sins [RSV: set forth your case], that you may be proved right' (Is 43:25-26). After your repentance, God makes no delay. You have spoken your sin and you are justified; you have been sorry and you are pardoned. It is not a question of time. It is the penitent's disposition which puts out sin.[16]

The same sermon uses an even more profound argument to reassure sinners without relaxing the fervor of the just.

God everywhere shows himself strict with the just
and lenient with sinners . . . . O what great exactitude toward the just! O what great tolerance with
the delinquent! He acts thus in a variety of ways,
not because he himself changes, but to make a profitable distribution of his goodness. If he were to
frighten the sinner who persists in his sins, he
would push him to discouragement and despair.
Were he to make the just man blessed, he would
slacken the nerve of his virtue, making him care-
less, since he would already consider himself
assured of his happiness. That is why he takes pity
on the sinner and makes the just man tremble:
'Great and terrible above all that are round about
him' (Ps 89:7); and, 'The Lord is good to all'
(Ps 145:9). Terrible, then, to all those around him.
And who would these be, if not the saints? In fact,
David says, 'A God feared in the council of the
holy ones, great and terrible above those that are
round about him'. If he sees someone fall he
stretches out his loving hand, but if he sees him
standing he uses fear. That is the work of justice
and equitable judgement. He fortifies the just man
through fear and lifts up the sinner through love
for men. Do you wish to know his timely goodness,
his helpful and fitting harshness? Then pay close
attention, do not fail to grasp the sublimity of this
consideration . . . .

There follows the story of the sinful woman of whom Jesus
said, 'Her sins, which are many, are forgiven, because she
loved much'. The text then adds, 'Yet Miriam, the sister of
Moses, is condemned to leprosy for a little murmuring'.
And there are further examples in support of the same thesis.

The conclusion to be drawn from all this is surely that
no-one ever has the right to despair, but neither may anyone
imagine himself dispensed from the remembrance of his

faults. These two attitudes converge precisely in compunction. Tears wipe out sin, but forgiveness never dries the
source of tears.

Many spiritual writers have considered and commented on
the expression 'baptism of tears'. Among the Syrians there is
James of Saroug who, like Saint Ephrem, seems never to have
been speaking of the sacrament. A sinner is present at the
liturgy. What will he do at the moment of communion, when
the priest proclaims, 'Holy things for the holy'?

> At that terrible moment weep for your sins and
> ask for mercy from God. With a contrite heart,
> saddened with its malice, shed tears and wash the
> stains of your soul. At that moment run to the
> baptism of tears and by that means purify and ex-
> piate the sins you have committed. Say to the
> Father, 'I have offended much and my foolishness
> has been great . . . ' . One only washes vessels in
> water, and it is only in tears that sins can be
> removed from the soul. Ten thousand talents would
> not wash the wickedness from a soul, as do the
> drops of tears, flowing from the eyes.[17]

Saint John Chrysostom had mentioned almsgiving as another
way of obtaining forgiveness. James of Saroug falls upon
an ingenious way of explaining its efficacy.

> You have no tears? Buy tears from the poor. You
> have no sadness? Call the poor to moan with you.
> If your heart is hard and has neither sadness nor
> tears, with alms invite the needy to weep with
> you. The exercise of pity is a great thing; it pro-
> cures tears for approaching God. Almsgiving is a
> fine thing in the one who gives it, but it is agree-
> able to God only through the tears of poverty.
> Compassion is a pure, a choice gift. Call the poor,
> that they may appease your Lord with their
> tears . . . . Provide yourself with the water of tears,
> and may the poor come to help you put out the

fire in which you are perishing. The greatest fire
can only be put out with tears. The pouring of
tears is a shower which extinguishes it, that terrible
fire which menaces criminals.[18]

Repentance, then, was as easy for James of Saroug as it was
for Chrysostom: 'You, purify yourself, and sanctify yourself;
that is easy for you to do. You can make your own baptism
flow from yourself, and you will be purified. All the waves
of the immense ocean would not wash you as would these
streams which the heart sends to the eyes.'[19]

Isaac of Nineveh went so far as to put baptism of tears
above the other baptism. The sacrament gives a foretaste, but
compunction gives us the charism.[20] Nor is it any longer
merely a question of remission of sins: 'If you truly seek,
you will find that true service in the fear of God is repentance. We have spoken of spiritual understanding on this
earth; it is that of which we have received a foretaste in
baptism. We receive the gift in repentance . . . '.[21] Isaac has a
complete philosophy of tears, one to which we will return. In
the letter attributed to Isaac in the Greek version, but which
is by Philoxenus of Mabboug,[22] we encounter the severity of
Saint Gregory Nazianzen: 'Baptism pardons freely, and
requires nothing but faith. Repentance, after baptism, is not
free, but requires exhausting effort, the afflictions of compunction, tears, prolonged weeping. It gives pardon on this
condition.'[23]

Saint Theodore the Studite, on the vigil of Epiphany,
exhorts 'his fathers, his brothers, and his children' to take
daily profit from this baptism, since it depends only on us.

Let us go in the spirit to the Jordan, and there let
us see the Great Light [remember that baptism is
called *photismos,* illumination], our Christ, bap-
tised. Let us kiss his fleeting traces in the water.
Let us no more return to the shades of sin, but let
us go forth and walk with him as true followers.
And first let us receive baptism with him, I mean

the baptism of tears, for it is in truth an ever shining purgatory. From our depths come the waves.
We too have a Jordan, illuminated as we are by the
flow of compunction. Let us follow Christ each
day . . . .[24]

Without naming baptism, these writers generally ascribe
baptismal power to tears. Thus Saint Barsanuphius, when he
was asked, 'How can I wash away my stains?' replied, 'If you
wish to wash your stains, wash them with tears, for they
do indeed wash every spot.'[25]

In another letter, evidently inspired by the saying of Peter
the Pionite,[26] Barsanuphius goes him one better:

True tears, accompanied with compunction, become a man's slave, unfailingly subject to him. The
man who has tears will not fall in any battle. They
even efface past faults and wash away stains. Ceaselessly, they keep the man who has obtained them
in the name of God. They banish laughter and
dissipation; they maintain an uninterrupted *penthos*. They are the shield off of which the flaming
arrows of the devil ricochet (Eph 6:16). He who
possesses them will fear no war, even if he is among
such people as prostitutes, for compunction is
with us in combat.[27]

The old men already knew this sovereign power of tears:

An old man said, 'Every sin that a man commits is
outside of the body, whereas a fornicator sins
against his own body (1 Cor 6:18). In the same
way, every good work that a man does is outside
of his body, whereas he who weeps purifies his
soul and his body, for tears coming from on high
wash the whole body and sanctify it.[28]

It is hard to imagine the purity in store for one who
administers to himself such a wonderful baptism daily or
rather, continually, since *penthos* can and must be perpetual. First he obtains forgiveness for sins committed before

conversion; this is an easy matter. Then, day by day and almost step by step, he will shake off the unavoidable dust of daily faults. These, moreover, will diminish steadily in number and gravity, as compunction cures the passions, those diseases of the soul of which faults are the symptoms. Saint Anthony had already made this point,[29] one which emerges from all these texts which present tears as the universal panacea. For anyone approaching the limits of perfection, the supreme temptation is the thought of pride, along with terrible desires to blaspheme. What is the remedy? Again, tears. Evagrius writes:

> In the Lord, concerning the words of a demon who puts forth in us unspeakable blasphemies— I could not write them—against the Lord. It is enough to shake heaven and earth, for this demon enters unashamedly into our irascible part, and utters enormous blasphemies against God and his holy angels. Those who have been tempted by him will know what I mean. Now at the hour of this temptation we should turn to fasting, spiritual reading and incessant prayers offered with tears.[30]

Of course we know that the demon of pride springs up when all the others have been defeated, profiting from our victory itself to whisper to us that it is all our doing.[31] Yet tears are more powerful than he. In a very short sentence Saint Ammonas sums up the doctrine of the Fathers on the curative power of *penthos*: 'Imperturbably, *penthos* removes all defects'.[32]

No-one had a higher concept of the baptism of tears than Symeon the New Theologian. He saw in it the true baptism of the Spirit, the great *photismos,* that illumination by which a man becomes all light.[33] The New Theologian must surely have read Isaac of Nineveh. In any case, he certainly noticed these effects of sanctification and illumination in his spiritual father, Simeon the Studite. Simeon too has left a short work in which praise of tears plays the chief role:

All [that is written in this book], brother, is [written] to promote compunction. You must carry it out with endurance, contrition of heart and thanksgiving, since these things bring tears and destroy passions . . . . If you do this, you will free yourself entirely from old habits, perhaps even from the first suggestions ($\pi\rho o\sigma\beta o\lambda a\iota$) of bad thought.[34] [Not to feel even these entirely innocent suggestions is clearly the height of *apatheia*.] Darkness normally gives way to light (baptism: $\phi\omega\tau\iota\sigma\mu os$) and shadows to the sun . . . . For, when the intellect is purified by a multitude of tears, it also receives the illumination of divine light.[35]

The author of these lines spoke from experience. After his death, his disciple, the New Theologian, addressed to him one day, and solemnly, this prayer: 'Saint Simeon, having become conformed to the image of Jesus Christ through the participation of the Holy Spirit, invested with the shining robe of *apatheia* thanks to a long *ascesis,* washed in your own tears, so copious as to equal the font of baptism . . . ' . [86] When Nicetas Stethatos put this prayer in writing, he certainly assumed that his readers would recognize, in passing, expressions of Saint Gregory the Theologian.

It is fitting to end this chapter with the beautiful prayer of a Syrian mystic whose works are unfortunately still unedited, John Saba, otherwise known as John of Dalyatha.[37] Three of his sermons, translated into Greek, passed into some manuscripts under the name of Isaac of Nineveh; from these we are fortunate enough to possess a Latin version.[38]

When we have conceived the desire to flee from the world and to become strangers to worldly men, there is nothing like mourning and sorrow of heart, with discretion, to separate us from the world, mortify our passions, and waken us to spiritual things. On the other hand, there is nothing like laughter and dissipation to lead us back into the

world and its inhabitants, its drunkards and volup-
tuaries, to separate us from the treasures of wisdom and the knowledge of God's secrets. These
vices are the machinations of the demon of lust....
Cry, then, give voice to groans and anxiety....
Flood your cheeks with the tears of your eyes,
that the Holy Spirit may rest on you and wash you
from the stains of your malice. Propitiate God
through your tears, that he may come to you.
Invite Mary and Martha to teach you the words of
mourning (πενθικὰς φωνάς). Cry to the Lord:

'Lord Jesus Christ our God, who wept over
Lazarus and poured on him tears of sadness and
compassion, accept the tears of my bitterness.
Through your passion heal my passions, through
your wounds bring remedies to my wounds, through
your blood purify my blood and mingle with my
body the perfume of your body which gives life.
May the gall which your enemies gave you to drink
sweeten my soul and dispel the bitterness poured
into it by the adversary. May your body, stretched
on the wood of the cross, speed towards you my
mind, so dragged down by demons. May your
head, which you laid on the cross, lift up again
my head, buffeted by enemies. May your most
holy hands, nailed to the cross by infidels, raise
me from the gulf of perdition towards you, as your
holy mouth promised (Jn 12:32). May your face,
which received blows and spitting from wretched
men, make my face to shine, deformed as it is by
iniquities. May your soul, which you gave up to
your Father on the cross, lead me to you by your
grace. I have no heart in mourning to seek you
with, I have neither repentance nor compunction,
which bring the children back to their inheritance.
Lord, I have no tears. My mind is clouded with

earthly cares, and cannot lift its gaze to you in sadness. My heart has grown cold in a multitude of temptations, and cannot warm itself with the tears of your love. But you, Lord Jesus Christ, treasure of all riches, grant me perfect repentance and a sorrowing heart, that I may seek you with all my heart, for apart from you I will have no riches. Give me therefore, O good one, your grace. May the Father from whose bosom you went forth outside of time, from all eternity, renew in me the features of your image. I have abandoned you; do not abandon me. I have gone out from your house; please go out to seek me and bring me into your pasture. Number me with the sheep of your chosen flock and feed me with them from the store of your divine mysteries . . . . ' [39]

## IX

## THE EFFECTS OF *PENTHOS:* BEATITUDE

FAR FROM DRYING UP the source of tears, certainty of forgiveness opens up a new and more abundant spring. There will always be sorrow, because the thought of lost salvation does not disappear even at the upper edges of the soul's ascent, yet above jagged clouds will shine the dawn of paradise. Even in this life, evangelical beatitude will give a first taste of its eternal promise. Joy will penetrate tears and transfigure a face which still retains its gravity. Man will not cease to consider himself a sinner; he will even do so with renewed intensity, bearing witness to the truth as well as to the love of God. The profane experience no more than an intermittent and superficial peace, coming between bouts of unsatisfied desires, whereas the ascetic, purified of his passions, will enjoy a true peace, the result of restored spiritual health. 'Now this profound peace is accompanied by humility, compunction, tears, an immense love for God and a boundless zeal for the practice of virtue.'[1]

We will understand our authors better when we remember that, among the passions to overcome, they include that of sadness. From the first moment of its presence in the soul, compunction fights against this enemy; the virtue will develop only as it checks the vice more and more, finally exterminating it by cutting off the sustenance furnished it by the seven other 'deadly thoughts'.[2] The first result of this will be a sense of well-being which is primarily negative: absence of anxiety, disappointments, nameless fears, rebellion against fate or against God's will. The Christian, however, will be content neither with the philosopher's calm nor the Moslem's resignation. He will pass from this human serenity to the heavenly peace which 'exults in the heart' because it results from a cause which reason cannot know. This will not yet be the joy of heaven, but in some sense the earthly paradise reopening its doors. His disposition is at once complex and simple; in the higher unity of God's love it combines feelings which had once seemed incompatible. He has the sense not only of having sinned but of *being* a sinner, and the confidence—almost the observable certainty—of having entered into God's grace. He has the overwhelming euphoria of a sick man amazed at finding himself cured, while in his limbs he still carries the physiological memory of his illness. Only one who has experienced sickness can have the conscious enjoyment of health. Ὁ ἀσθενήσας αὐτὸς ἄγνω τὴν ὑγίειαν.[3] It is from having suffered estrangement from God, to the point of tears, that he will tremble the more with joy at nearness to him. He knows that he is still unworthy of this divine tenderness which enfolds him; he even grasps more and more clearly the contrast between what he deserves and what he is receiving. Is it then strange that his feelings are moved in spite of themselves, and that now his tears flow, not because he has wanted them but because, whether he wants them or not, he can no longer hold them back?[4]

Χαροποιὸν πένθος (grace-making *penthos*). In these two words John Climacus, as a man who knows his sources (and he was far more erudite than has been supposed), condenses the whole doctrine of the Fathers. Of course many of them, perhaps most, avoid insisting on this new aspect of their beloved *penthos.* Yet it surely takes nothing away from their heroism to say that they would not have spoken so highly of tears had they not found in them so great an attraction. Mme Lot-Borodine had one of her accustomed happy insights when she entitled an article 'The Mystery of Tears'.[5] Like all mysteries, especially in antiquity, this one is subject to the law of the secret. Spiritual *finesse* and discretion are

synonymous. There is in fact a very simple way of recon-
ciling the duty of preaching compunction with the niceties
of humility. From one end of the scale to the other, from
the newly converted assassin[6] to the ecstatic transported
to Calvary and the company of the Virgin Mary, the same
name will designate the cause of tears: *penthos* or *catanyxis.*

'Why do you weep Father?' 'I am weeping for my sins.'
*Abstrahentis non est mendacium.* It is the truth, but not the
whole truth. Mental reservation of this sort sets Saint Arsenius
and his disciples at ease. There is no need to hide one's tears,
since they proclaim no more than that we are sinners. We
can be glad, then, that some preachers and biographers, no
doubt because of a little personal experience, have pierced
the mystery so jealously guarded by the 'blessed mourners'.
These latter would not have contradicted such writers,
although they might perhaps have protested against a revelation forbidden both by humility and by that stern modesty
of the most despotic of all loves.

It is not then from the most ancient spiritual writers that
we gather the greatest number of testimonies on the joy of
*penthos*—only fleeting indications which require interpreta-
tion. Thus, when Evagrius ends his *Chapters on Prayer* by
saying, 'When in your prayer you have arrived above all
other joy, then at last, in truth, you will have found
prayer',[7] we must remember that the path to this happiness
began with tears, and that at mid-point we were still being
reminded of the constant necessity of weeping for our
sins.[8] It is clear then that compunction ends in beatitude.
The moral writings of Saint Ephrem might be divided into
two categories: exhortations to repentance, and songs of
triumph, 'woes' and 'blesseds'. Yet the real Saint Ephrem is
unconcerned with psychology. Eschatology is the controlling
idea in his work. Eternal hope is enough for his happiness
on earth. Saint John Chrysostom came a little closer to our
level, trying to draw his hearers to compunction with the
bait of more immediate consolations.

Blessed are those who are in mourning, and woe to those who laugh, says Christ. How then can Saint Paul tell us to rejoice always? Not in contradiction to Christ; heaven forbid! 'Woe to those who laugh', said Christ, meaning by that the laughter of this world concerning present things. He blessed mourners, not those who are simply in mourning over the loss of their possessions, but those who have compunction and who weep over their own misdeeds, those who reflect on their own sins or even on those of another. Now this joy is not contrary to that mourning; it is even born from it. He who weeps for his evil deeds and admits them is in joy. To put the same thing in another way: it is possible to be in mourning for one's own sins and in joy because of Christ.[9]

There is only one consolation, that the Lord is near to hear our prayers and receive our thanks.[10]

Nearness to Christ! John Chrysostom knows well, because his Saint Paul told him so, that there is nothing more highly to be desired. Nonetheless, when he hears this great lover of Christ reminding the elders at Ephesus of the tears which he wept day and night for three years for their salvation (Ac 20:31), Chrysostom perceives something yet greater:

These eyes [of Saint Paul] saw paradise, they saw the third heaven, yet I do not praise them for this contemplation as much as for the tears through which he saw Christ. It is surely happiness to see Christ, and Paul himself boasts of it: 'Have I not seen Jesus our Lord?' (1 Cor 9:1). Still, there is more happiness in weeping in the way we have said. Many shared this sight, but Christ calls happy those who did not share it: 'Blessed are those who have not seen and have believed' (Jn 20:29). If it is more necessary for the salvation of others to remain in the world than to leave it, it is also more necessary to sorrow over them than to see Christ. If, more than being with him, it is preferable to be in Gehenna because of him . . . ('For I could wish that I myself were accursed and cut off from Christ for the sake of my brethren' (Rom 9:3), it is all the more preferable to weep for his sake [for the salvation of others].[11]

Saint Nilus shows himself a good disciple of John Chrysostom when he writes

Lamentation over one's sins brings a very sweet sadness and a bitterness which tastes like honey, being seasoned with a marvellous hope. That is why it nourishes the body, causes the depths of the soul to shine with joy, enriches the heart and causes our whole being to thrive. How right David was to sing. 'Tears have become my bread day and night' (Ps 41:4).[12]

The reflections of Abba Isaiah are less medical but more profound:

Brother, mount a vigilant guard against the spirit which brings sadness to a man. This sets off numerous diabolical mechanisms which will not stop until your strength is sapped. Sadness according to God, on the other hand, is a joy, the joy of seeing yourself in God's will . . . . Sadness according to God does not weigh on the soul, but says to it, 'Do not be afraid! Up! Return!' God knows that man is weak, and strengthens him.[13]

The specialty of Saint Ammonas, a disciple of the great Anthony, was endlessly to praise the wonders of the divine power ($\theta\epsilon\ddot{\iota}\kappa\dot{\eta}$ $\delta\acute{v}\nu\alpha\mu\iota\varsigma$), repose ($\alpha\nu\acute{\alpha}\pi\alpha\upsilon\sigma\iota\varsigma$), lightness ($\dot{\epsilon}\lambda\alpha\phi\rho\acute{o}\tau\eta\varsigma$), divine warmth ($\theta\acute{\epsilon}\rho\mu\eta$ $\theta\epsilon\ddot{\iota}\kappa\dot{\eta}$), and liberty ($\dot{\epsilon}\lambda\epsilon\upsilon\theta\epsilon\rho\acute{\iota}\alpha$), which result from the labor of those who valiantly practice 'spiritual cultivation'.

This is the pearl of the Gospel which was bought by the man who had sold all his goods (Mt 13:45), it is the treasure which was hidden in the field and caused great joy to the man who found it.[14]

Here is the ancestry of this glorious plant:

Fear produces tears, and tears joy. Joy brings strength, through which the soul will be fruitful in everything. If God sees such fine fruit, he receives it as an odor of sweetness; he rejoices with his angels and gives it a watchman to protect it in all its ways, leading it to its place of rest so that Satan can do nothing against it. As long as the devil sees the watchman, that is, the virtue which surrounds the soul, he flees in fear of approaching the man, respectful of the virtue which covers him. Therefore, dearly beloved in the Lord, you whom I love because I know that you are dear to God, acquire this virtue in yourselves so that Satan may fear you, to become wise in all your works, and that the sweetness of grace may help and increase your fruit. For the sweetness of the spiritual charism is sweeter than honey and the honeycomb (Ps 18:11). There is no great number of monks or virgins who have known this great sweetness of grace, only a few here and there. Most have not acquired divine virtue because they have not cultivated it, and so the Lord has not given it to them. He gives it to those who cultivate it, being no respecter of persons (Ac 10:34), and to those who do this, he gives it from generation to generation.[15]

Elsewhere Ammonas establishes a different order of succession:

Solitude produces *ascesis* and tears, tears produce fear, fear produces humility and watchfulness, watchfulness produces charity, and charity renders the soul healthy and impassible. Now man understands that after all these things he is not far from God.[16]

This apparent contradiction points to a kind of reciprocal causality: fear produces tears, tears increase fear, and fear redoubles tears. The important thing is to set out on the task for once and for all.

Ammonas usually calls this 'spiritual charism' the Spirit. There is no other way of receiving it than through repentance:

> The Spirit enters into no souls but those which are entirely purified from their old ways, for he is holy and cannot enter into an impure soul. That is why Our Lord did not give it to the apostles before they had been purified. That is why he told them, 'If I go, I will send you the Paraclete, the Spirit of truth, who will guide you into all the truth' (Jn 16:7, 13). From Abel and Enoch to this day, this Spirit gives itself to the souls of the just who have entirely purified themselves. The other souls receive not this but the spirit of repentance which calls all souls and washes them from their impurity. When it has completely purified them, it sends them to the Holy Spirit which endlessly pours out on them softness and sweetness, as Levi has said, 'Who has known the sweetness of the Spirit, except those in whom it has dwelt?'[17]

The Spirit is the Paraclete, *consolator optimus*. The doctrine of Ammonas can thus be summed up in this phrase attributed to Saint Ephrem: 'He who wishes to be consoled must give himself up to *penthos*'.[18] How could one be anything but consoled, when 'mourning' gives us all that is required for the purest happiness?

> We will therefore have joyful faces, exulting in the Holy Spirit over the Lord's gifts, but weeping and sorrowful in thought, beseeching God to keep us from every kind of evil, that we be not deprived of the kingdom of heaven and the good things which he has prepared for those who have known how

to please him. Mourning builds up and keeps.
Mourning cleanses the soul through tears and
reestablishes it in its purity. Mourning produces
temperance, cuts away passions and practises the
virtues. What more can I say? Mourning is beatified
by God and consoled by the angels.[19]

We have already criticized Nicetas Stethatos who, in his
search for a more precise vocabulary, put undue restraints on
the meaning of *catanyxis,* reserving it as he did to charismatic
compunction.[20] The Greek tradition scarcely knows this
narrow sense, either for *catanyxis,* as can be seen in Saint
John Chrysostom, or for *penthos,* as is evident in Saint John
Climacus. The ancients had a good reason for refusing this
restriction. To admit it would have involved a dangerous
obstacle to humility and hence to compunction itself. It
must not be forgotten that the highest compunction cannot
exist without the thought of lost salvation. Too many dis-
tinctions, however necessary for the clarification of concepts,
can produce unfortunate practical consequences. There is no
question, for example, but that theological speculation gained
immensely from the use of the terms 'natural' and 'supernatural'. Once this distinction passes into christian life, however, it tends to masquerade as a real opposition, as though
one had to *choose* between the natural and the supernatural.
From there it is but a step either to Jansenist pessimism,
where nature is essentially hostile to grace, or to the
naturalism of those who flatter themselves on having 'super-
naturalized their affections'. The same problem arises concerning the terms 'ascetic' and 'mystic' and, to return to our
subject, the terms 'tears of repentance' and 'tears of compunction'.

When all this has been said, Nicetas Pectoratus is still
justified in distinguishing two *degrees*:

Tears of repentance are to be distinguished from
tears shed through divine compunction. The former
are like a flood which carries off all the dikes of

sin, while the latter fall on the soul as the rain upon the grass and as the showers upon the herb (Dt 32:3), causing knowledge to grow up for the harvest and multiplying its grains. All tears do not necessarily come from *catanyxis;* the two are quite different. Tears come from repentance and the remembrance of past strayings of the soul; as though from fire and boiling water, they are for the purification of the heart. *Catanyxis* comes from on high, from the divine dew of the Spirit. It consoles and refreshes the soul which has just entered with fervor into the abyss of humility, which has received the contemplation of inaccessible light, and which cries to God in joy, with David, 'We went through fire and through water, yet you have brought us forth to a spacious place' (Ps 66:12).[21]

Having noted Isaac of Nineveh's influence on Symeon the New Theologian, we should now observe it on Nicetas Stethatos:[22]

What are the exact signs which begin to show evidence of the hidden fruits of man's work, those interior to the soul?

[*Reply*] When he is judged worthy of the gift of abundant and unconstrained tears. Tears are placed as a frontier for the mind between corporeity and spirituality, between the state of passion and the state of purity. As long as one has not received this gift, the work of his service remains in the outward man and there is no way that he can acquire even the smallest sense of the service hidden in the spiritual man. But when he begins to leave the corporeity of this world and to pass into the realm which is within visible nature,[23] he will immediately arrive at this grace of tears. From the very first stage of this hidden life his tears will begin,

and they will lead him to the perfect love of God.
And when he arrives there he will have such an
abundance of them that he will drink them with
his food and drink, so perpetual and profuse are
they. That is a certain sign for the mind of its
withdrawal from this world and of its perception of
the spiritual world. To the extent that it approaches this world here, tears will diminish, and
when he is totally immersed in it, he will also be
totally deprived of tears. That is the sign that he is
buried in passions.[24]

The following text of Isaac seemed so important to Paul
Evergetinos that he inserted it in his long chapter on
*penthos*.[25] It is certain that his contemporary, Nicetas
Stethatos, had also read it:

Some tears are searing and some make us thrive.
All tears which come from repentance and distress
of heart, flowing because of sins, dry up the body
and burn it. It is not even rare that lesions of the
brain are produced by their effusion. It is to these
tears that a man must necessarily come as a first
stage, and they open to him a door to the second
stage, which is much more excellent, being the sign
of having received mercy. What is this sign? Tears
which flow from knowledge make the body
thrive.[26] They flow by themselves; there is no
constraint. They even fatten the body and trans-
form the expression of the face. For, it is written,
a glad heart makes a cheerful countenance (Prov
15:13). They spread over the whole face in the
silence of thoughts. Thus the body receives a sort
of food, and our countenance is cheerful. He who
has experienced these two kinds of tears will
understand.[27]

The Greek of Theotokis omits the last two sentences, and
Evergetinos replaces them with this reflection: 'If, then, we

desire to receive the second type, let us apply ourselves with all our power to the first, and before long we will obtain the others through the grace of God'.

Not having had these experiences, we are reduced to looking elsewhere for fuller explanations. Isaac supplies them for us as clearly as he can in his allegorical language:

On those who walk in the way of solitude.

When do they begin to know, to however small a degree, where they have arrived in their labors on this boundless sea of the solitary life? Is there any assurance to be had that their effort has begun to bear fruit?

I will tell you something, and do not laugh, because I tell the truth, and do not doubt my word, for I have received this teaching from trustworthy sources. It will be useless for you to hang on the pupils of your eyes until you receive tears; do not think that you will get anywhere that way. Your inward man is still in the service of the world; you still act as a worldling. It is in your outward man that you strive to do God's work, and your inward man is still without fruit. It will begin to bear fruit at the moment I have said. When you arrives at the zone of tears, know then that your mind has gone out of the person of this world, that it has placed its feet on the road to a new world, and that it has begun to breathe the wonderful air from above. Now it begins to shed tears, for the labor pains of spiritual birth are becoming intense. Grace, the mother of all, is eager to give mystic birth to the soul, the image of God in the light of the world to come. When the time of delivery comes, the mind begins thenceforth to experience something from above, as a subtle breath which the child receives within his mother's womb. But since he cannot bear what is not familiar to him, his body is moved to cry tears mixed with a joy which surpasses the sweetness of honey. As this inward child grows, tears increase. The flow of tears takes place from the very moment that the mind begins to make itself limpid. By this I mean the flowing of tears proper to the degree of which I speak; I am not concerned with that partial flowing which comes from time to time. This occasional consolation comes to anyone who serves God in silence, whether through intellectual contemplation, through the words of Scripture, or through application to the prayer of petition. What I mean is that total flowing which is ceaseless day and night. It comes to him who through the exactitude of his life has found the truth in solitude, to such an extent that his eyes become sources of water for the space of two years or even more. That comes in a period of mystical transition. After tears you will enter into the peace of thoughts, whence you will enter into the divine rest of which Paul speaks in his characteristically enigmatic way. From this region of peace the mind will begin to see hidden things. Then the Holy Spirit begins to unveil to it the things of heaven, while God remains in you, increasing the fruits of the spirit. From now on you will become aware of the transformation which all nature must receive when God makes all things new, but obscurely and as in an enigma.

Then Isaac mentions his sources: meditation on Scripture, the sayings of trustworthy people, and a little experience as well. Then he continues:

Listen to something else which I will tell you as I learned it from a mouth which does not lie. As soon as you enter into this region of the peace of thoughts, then the violence of tears is removed from you and you come to what remains in the limits of measure. There is the exact truth in a few words; it is confirmed and believed by the whole Church, by those of her children who are experts and controversialists.[28]

This, then, is where tears lead: to perfect peace, which is the prelude to the highest contemplation, to the revelation of heavenly mysteries, to a marvellous transformation of the whole being. I have no doubt but that Nicetas Stethatos was inspired by these texts.

He must have read them all the more eagerly because his master Symeon had already done so. For the Byzantines of the tenth and eleventh centuries, Isaac was still an almost entirely new author, in any case unknown to the last great spiritual writer, Maximus the Confessor. Looking elsewhere, one could find a similar meaning in the sayings of Ammonas cited above. Saint Maximus had seen spiritual enlightenment in the 'wine of compunction'.[29] Saint Barsanuphius, too, had distinguished between intermittent and perpetual compunction, without however reserving the name *catanyxis* to the latter: 'Brother, the tears and *catanyxis* which you now have are not authentic, because they come and go. True tears, accompanied with *catanyxis,* become man's slave, inseparably subject to him. He who has them will not succumb in any war.'[30] The cenobite on whom this grace falls is ready for the life of a hesychast, having attained the *apatheia* which will make it possible for him to pray continually. For him there will be no more 'canon'; the Holy Spirit becomes his guide:

> Rejoice in the Lord, brother, rejoice in the Lord, beloved; rejoice in the Lord, my co-heir. Pray always, as befits this level of *apatheia.* Then you will recognize the coming of the Spirit, who teaches all things. And if all things, then prayer. The apostle says, 'For we do not know how to pray as we ought, but the Spirit himself intercedes for us with sighs too deep for words' (Rom 8:26).

> Why should I have spoken to you earlier of the
> edifices of Rome, when you had not yet been
> there? A hesychast no longer has any canon. Be
> like a man who eats and drinks as much as he
> wants. Thus, when the idea of reading occurs to
> you and you see compunction in your heart, read
> as long as you can. The same things holds for
> psalmody. With all your strength retain thankful-
> ness and the *Kyrie eleison,* and do not fear, for
> God's charisms are immutable.[31]

In the spirituality of the Evagrian tradition we will say
then that *penthos* is the secret of contemplation. In the less
intellectualist tradition of ascetics such as the 'old men', we
will say that it is the path to union with God. The termino-
logy may vary, but the teaching is the same. All agree that
compunction leads to the 'highest thing to be desired'.

Let us return for a moment to an idea of Isaac of Nineveh.
There is a period, he says, in which tears are particularly
abundant; after it they find their proper level. This is a period
of transition from the mental to the spiritual level. Man is
composed of body, soul, and spirit; from this comes the
division of the christian life into three degrees: somatic,
psychic (mental), and pneumatic (spiritual). 'The second
degree is midway between the passionate stage and spirituality.'[32]

> This is the work of the heart. It is to be carried
> on without respite in meditation on the great
> judgement to come, in a perpetual prayer of the
> heart, in consideration of God's providence and
> care for the world, for individuals as well as for
> species . . . . Through the work of the way which is
> called mental, the heart is refined and detached
> from corrupting involvements or unnatural pas-
> sions.[33]

From the fervor [of this second stage] comes

vision through grace, and thus is born the effusion
of tears. At first this is partial, with tears coming
to a man numerous times in a single day. After
that he comes to uninterrupted pouring forth.
Through tears the soul receives peace of thoughts;
through peace of thoughts it rises to perfect purity
of the mind. Thanks to a perfectly pure mind, man
comes to the point of seeing hidden things, for
purity results from the pacification which puts an
end to wars. After that, the intellect attains what
corresponds to the flood which the prophet Ezekiel
saw, a flood which typifies the three degrees of the
soul on the way to divine life. Of these degrees,
there is no going beyond the third.[34]

'Water ankle-deep, water knee-deep, water up to the loins, a
river that I could not pass through.' Such are the degrees
of tears.

But then, why does this flood end by receding? If it is
because the soul enters on a spiritual state, why should not
this lowering proceed all the way to complete dryness?
Nowhere, at least in what remains of his works, does Isaac
say a word about a total disappearance of tears. Only a few
years ago there would have been no answer to these questions.
Today, though, we know where Isaac found his division of
three ways. It is in the work of a writer until recently confused with John of Lycopolis, but who is in fact a Syrian
author of the fourth or fifth century.[35] Until he is more
precisely identified, we will call him John the Solitary. His
theory of tears is so original that the passage in which he
expounds it must, despite its length, be given in full.

Let us come then to the distinction of tears
poured forth, to see what thoughts provoke them
in the understanding, according to the three
classes.

Well, the tears of the bodily man, even when he
weeps before God in prayer, are provoked by the

following thoughts: anxiety about his poverty, remembrance of his misfortunes, concern for his children, suffering coming from his oppressors, care for his house, remembrance of his dead relatives, and other such things. The continual harrassment of these thoughts augments his sadness, and from sadness tears are born.

At the mental stage, tears in prayer are provoked by the following thoughts: fear of judgement, a conscience burdened by sins, remembrance of God's goodness to himself, meditation on death, the promise of things to come. Through persistence in these thoughts, there is an inward awakening of the emotion of tears. Now if there are other people around this man, unless he exercises extraordinary vigilance, his tears will not be caused by these reflections. He will begin to be tainted with the passion for human glory, as he considers their number and his presence among them, and then it will be human respect which excites his tears through vainglory.

The tears of the spiritual man are determined by these thoughts: admiration of God's majesty, stupefaction before the depth of his wisdom, the glory of the world to come, the straying of men, and other such things. Through persistence in these thoughts, tears spring up before God. Moreover, these tears come from no sadness, but from an intense joy. These tears are born from joy in the same way that many persons, seeing their friends after a long absence, weep with joy at their sight. There are also tears of the spiritual man which come from sadness, and here is their cause: when he remembers men and thinks how they have strayed, he weeps as did our Lord entering Jerusalem, or again when it is said that he was afflicted by the heaviness of their heart;[36] or as Saint Paul says, 'I speak of them even with tears' (Phil 3:18), or again as it is written of him in Acts that for three years he had not ceased to weep (Ac 20:31). Yet note that these tears were not caused by a feeling or mood, but by thoughts of the soul on the straying of men or on their sufferings and miseries, or because they were begging help from heaven. The spiritual man is not quick to weep, given his habitual joy; if he does weep, it is because he is moved by mental thoughts, as I have said. Take Simon Peter: because of the remembrance of his denial of Our Lord, he wept bitterly. In fact, each time Our Lord wept, the evangelist noted which thoughts made him weep; for example, when he looked into the dispositions of men and considered their dead heart, he wept over them. On the other hand, when man's mind is in the region of the spirit he does not weep, just as angels do not weep. Moreover, if tears came from a spiritual state, the just would always weep in the kingdom, since there they are spiritual. In spiritual conduct, therefore, there are no tears. In spiritual growth, then, what is the degree of him who weeps ceaselessly, if it be not that of the child who weeps ceaselessly? And just as the child, to the degree that he approaches the age of an adult, abstains from crying as he waits to arrive at an age when it will be improper to weep at all, so it is with him who persists in tears of all sorts. If God allows him to approach spiritual growth, to the extent that his understanding grows spiritually, he ceases to weep and is in joy. As for the one who has no inward sorrow and who is never moved in any way, he is in comparison with the spiritual man like a child not yet born in comparison with an adult at full manly stature.

One who is not yet born is entirely in the womb.
As for the man who has no sorrowful repentance
of soul, his whole mind is enclosed here below, and
cannot go out into the other world through
aspiration.[37]

If Isaac of Nineveh had read John the Solitary, which is
beyond doubt,[38] why did he not follow him completely in
this question of tears? First, because this teaching on the
ceasing of tears has scarcely another representative beyond
this mysterious hermit. Then too, Isaac checked his reading
against his own experience, a source which gave him no
knowledge of such a sublime state. He was too taken with
the sweetness of tears, and praised it too often, to admit that
tears might or even should entirely disappear. In any case, he
is never the least bit at odds with his source. The question
which still must be answered is whether it is possible from
our level to rise so high in the life of the spirit that we are
equal to the angels and saints in paradise. To this, John the
Solitary answers in the negative.[39] Isaac has therefore interpreted his master correctly in admitting a dimunition, but
not the total suppression of tears.

Nevertheless, we know at least one example of a man who
went beyond the limits fixed for mortals. His name is
Symeon, called the New Theologian. At least once he was
there where God wipes away every tear, where there is no
longer mourning or crying, in heaven, in the true heaven of
the elect and the angels.

One day, as he stood in very pure prayer, here is
what he saw: in his mind, the air began to shine.
Being within his cell, he seemed to be outside in
broad daylight, although it was at night, around
the first watch. A light as that of dawn began to
shine from on high—O marvellous visions of this
man!—the house and everything else vanished, and
he thought himself to be no longer in the house.
In a total ecstasy he fixed his whole mind on the

light which was approaching him. It grew, little
by little, making the air shine more and more, and
he felt himself going out, with his whole body,
from earthly things. As this light continued to
shine more and more brightly, and became above
him equal to the sun in its noon-day splendor, he
perceived that he was himself in the middle of the
light and completely filled with joy and tears by
the sweetness which was so nearly overwhelming
his entire body. He saw the light unite itself in an
extraordinary way with his flesh and little by little
penetrate his members. The amazing character of
this vision took him far from his previous contemplation; he had never seen anything like what
he saw happening within himself. Finally, then, he
saw this entire light gradually suffuse his entire
body, his heart and his entrails, so as to render him
all fire and light. And as had just happened with
the house, so now it made him lose the feeling of
shape, of posture, of thickness, of bodily appearance, *and he ceased to weep.* A voice came out
of the light which said, 'Thus must the saints be
transformed who will still be alive when the last
trumpet sounds'. Once they have entered into this
state, they will be carried up, as Saint Paul says
(1 Thess 4:17). A good many hours passed in this
way: the blessed one stood, never ceasing to sing
to God in mystical songs without any distraction
as he contemplated the glory which enfolded him,
the beatitude reserved eternally for the saints. He
then began to reason, and inwardly said to himself, 'Will I return to the original form of my body,
or will I remain as I am?' Scarcely had he made this
reflection than suddenly he realized that he was
still in his own body. He saw that it was this body
which, as we have said, had become totally light, a

light without form or shape, immaterial. He could
certainly feel that his body was present to him, yet
it was incorporeal in some way and spiritual. It
seemed to him to have neither weight nor thickness, and he was amazed to see himself incorporeal
in a body. Just then the light began again to speak
within him as it just had, saying, 'Such will be the
saints after the resurrection in the age to come,
incorporeally clothed with spiritual bodies, lighter,
more subtle, and more apt to rise, or thicker,
heavier, carried more to the earth. That is how the
place and rank of intimacy with God will vary for
each one'.[40]

Anyone whose critical temper is not completely removed
by this amazing account must content himself with lesser
stuff. To be sure, one has read elsewhere, in Origen and
Evagrius,[41] of the theory of spiritual bodies, and the light
without form or shape also awakens memories. The point is
that this is no longer a theory, but the actualization of a
theory. *Das Unzulängliche, hier wird's Ereignis.*[42] We are in
the Holy of Holies. John the Solitary had good reason to
repeat endlessly his refrain: all that relates to the summit of
the spiritual life belongs to the life which follows the resurrection.[43] Yet he had not considered the 'saints who, being
still alive when the last trumpet shall sound,' will undergo
that ineffable transformation without passing through death.
Now what will be done on the last day for the elect, cannot
God also, on a day he chooses, do in advance for a mystic?
In any case, what does it matter for now? The important
thing is that weeping ends in the kingdom of heaven, and
only there. The angels do not weep, says John the Solitary.
Isidore of Pelusium adds in his slightly gruff tone that they
do not laugh either.[44]

# EPILOGUE

A T THE END of this study several thoughts suggest
themselves. First, is there any need to apologize for
having undertaken it? Certainly not before the
worldly and the sceptical. We know what they would say.
They would speak, with Karl Höll, of *mönchliche Weichheit*,
of 'monastic softness, which in its panegyrics on tears expresses itself in terms unacceptable to us'.[1] 'To us'—that is,
Höll. Everyone is competent to form his own personal
impression, and Höll's is quite admissable as long as it is only
for himself. On one point, though, he has missed the mark:
monastic softness, tenderness, sensitivity. Why not 'femi-
nine' or 'childish'? We have only mentioned two women.
One of these, Saint Marina, forced herself to lead a totally
masculine form of life. The other, Saint Syncletica, was
worthy of her 'senatorial' name; she could give lessons to a
philosopher. Nor is *penthos* for the young. If ever men
proved their strength of character, it must be those of the
mettle of Arsenius, Ephrem, John Chrysostom and Symeon.
It is for Symeon the New Theologian that Höll had the least
respect, even though he had read the Life by Nicetas, where
he must have noticed that the biographer boasts, and with
reason, of the indomitable energy (τὸ ἀταπείνωτον τοῦ
φρονήματος) of his hero. To prove that compunction
weakens character, one would have to find examples elsewhere than in 'this stubborn champion of justice and
truth'.[2] The fact is that the lives of the saints, ancient and
modern, reveal a definite and close bond between the gift of
tears and firmness of will. One of the most extraordinary
phenomena of the will that ever was, according to the

157

Protestant Böhmer, may be found in Saint Ignatius Loyola.[3] How then explain that his spiritual journal notes so many tears, if these are signs of weakness? Compensation perhaps? The revenge of a downtrodden sensitivity? Not a bit of it. Then a mystery? Not even that. It is the easiest thing in the world to understand.

'I fear God, and I have no other fear'. *Servire Deo regnare est.* [To serve God is to reign.] Compunction frees us from passions which, even if they are labelled 'strong', are nonetheless the leaven of cowardice. Compunction presupposes the sacrifice of one's own will and produces attachment to the divine will whose calm and sovereign intransigence it communicates to man. If there is weakness, it is only before God. If there is 'softness' (*Weichheit*), it comes from that softness which Saint Irenaeus recommends as essential to God's creatures:

> Offer to him a heart that is soft and pliable. Keep the
> form in which the creator shaped you. Keep a good
> disposition, lest being hardened you lose the imprints
> of his fingers .... To make is proper to God's kind-
> ness, and to be made is proper to human nature ....
> If then you hand over to him what is yours, that is,
> faith and subjection, you will receive his craftsman-
> ship, and you will be a perfect work of God.[4]

The metaphysical quality of our created essence is passivity and receptivity. In relation to God, we are more childlike than children, more the 'frail sex' than women. Saint Ephrem gave such a great example and precept of compunction precisely because he had such a high idea of the divine majesty and pity.[5] At the revelation of such truths, pure spirits would simply fall into ecstasy. Since, in men who are both spirit and flesh, ecstasy provokes a physiological sense of being infinitesimal before majesty, and of being totally unworthy before love, are not emotion and tears natural, logical, inevitable? They could be avoided only through a lack of faith, intelligence, or 'humanity'. Ἀγριότης (savageness), said Evagrius, who was skilled in literature and philosophy.[6]

Even here, in the sanctuary, might we be blamed for having roused disagreeable old ghosts from the dust in which they were sleeping? To think so would be an insult to anyone who knows how highly the Lives of the Fathers have been esteemed in all times and places, not least in the Latin and Benedictine West. Denys Gorce has written on 'The Role of the *Vitae Patrum* in the Elaboration of the Benedictine Rule',[7] and similar studies could be made for all regions of Christianity. The most resonant voices among the Eastern saints would form a single choir to sing the praises of the 'Paradise of the Fathers'. Assuredly no-one, of those whose opinion carries weight, will object that now is the time for liturgy *rather than* asceticism, for expansion of the personality *rather than* turning inward, for great syntheses *rather than* dry erudition. This sort of 'either/or' runs against tradition, limits truth, and misses the point. Liturgy without asceticism? An old temptation:

> There was a brother at Scete who was zealous for
> the liturgy but negligent about the rest. One day
> Satan appeared to one of the old men and said,
> 'How wonderful! This monk is strangling me in a
> headlock, to prevent me from leaving him. He does
> everything I want, and yet he says to God at every
> hour, "Lord, deliver me from the Evil One".'[8]

Is turning inward opposed to expansion? Denis the Mystic (and Plotinus) taught that only introversion leads to ecstasy. As for syntheses which would make light of erudition, they will end sooner or later as does everything built on sand. Saint John Chrysostom had already had to deal with Christians who laughed at his tirades against laughter and his exhortations to weeping. He was not to be intimidated.

> Serve God with tears, that you may wash away
> your sins. I know that many jeer at us, saying,
> 'Right away, tears!' That is just the right moment

for them to shed some tears . . . . Vanity of vani-
ties, all is vanity. Let us turn to *penthos,* dearly
beloved, let us give ourselves up to mourning, that
we may indeed rejoice at the time of true joy. The
joy of this earth is necessarily mixed with sadness;
you will never find it in a pure state. The other joy
is true and without deceit; it contains no threat
of disappointment, no mixture with a foreign
element. That is the happiness which we must
enjoy, and which we are to pursue. Now there is
no other way of obtaining it than the habit of
choosing in this world what is profitable rather
than what is pleasant, of accepting small hardships
willingly and of bearing all the accidents of life
thankfully.[9]

If indeed this small book were called on to justify its
existence, it could say that it is in good company. Men of our
day, including a woman of great talent, have already written
on the 'problem of tears'.[10] If we have done so in our turn, it
is because these authors considered only one aspect of the
question and that, in our opinion, not the principal one.
Dom Steidle entitles his article, 'Tears. A mystical problem
in ancient monasticism'. One may of course limit one's subject in time, or consider only one side of it, that most
agreeable to our contemporaries. But is that really the way
to resolve the problem, if problem there be?

There is indeed one, but it is not primarily mystical. It is
first of all a problem of faith. Then, since real tears are
involved, it is a psychological, and even a physiological
problem. Then there is a slight, a very slight, question of
customs. Finally, in a few cases, there is a mystical problem.
We will have a word to say on each of these aspects, basing
ourselves as far as possible on the same authorities which we
have been citing until now. After all, they were concerned
with these questions long before scholars became interested
in them. We have no right to challenge their testimony, still

less to condemn them without having heard them plead
their case.

They need not, of course, justify the eccentricities of this
or that character deprived of the most necessary virtue of all,
discretion. 'Some have afflicted their bodies by asceticism,'
said Abba Anthony, 'but they lack discernment, and so they
are far from God.'[11] The same holds true for those few
flagellants who confused physical pain with 'the pain of the
heart'. We have already traced one example of this sanguinary
deception to its source, the same source for other tricks
which were invented to produce bogus *penthos*. This is that
strange and anonymous old man who permitted the obtaining
of tearful emotions through any sort of idle thought, only
surreptitiously to introduce the idea of compunction on its
heels. He was the same man who advised that one prolong
the enjoyment of tears as long as possible, heedless of any
control. This is a twisted hedonism, to which one might
aptly retort with Abba Poemen's saying, 'Teach your mouth
to say what is in your heart'.[12] The honesty of the Fathers,
even when crude or naive, knows nothing of these tortuous
shortcuts. They know only too well that there is but one way
to the goal, the straight way of renouncing one's own will.
This is the only means of pulling the soul's passions up by
the roots. Besides, how ancient are the sayings of this
worthy? They do not figure in the oldest collections, the
Alphabetic Series and the *Verba Seniorum*. The remainder, an
anonymous gathering, was always open to interpolations. It is
only in the twelfth century that we find an imitator of this
flagellant for the love of tears, Cyril of Philea.

Abba Isaiah, who died in 488, brings us back to the
authentic sense of tradition:

> Two monks lived at Caparbiana, on the outskirts
> of Gaza, in separate cells. One of them wept day
> and night. His neighbor said to him, 'Brother, don't
> you think that your weeping may be inspired by
> demons?' The brother replied, 'Forgive me, these

tears do not even allow me to eat'. The first
brother said, 'Why don't we go to Abba Isaiah?
You can tell him about this whole matter of
tears.' So they went and informed Abba Isaiah of
their problem through his disciple Peter. The old
man sent back to them this answer: 'It is from the
demons that these tears come. Have you not heard
what the Fathers say, that all which exceeds limits
is from the demons?'[13]

Ought the same message to have been sent to some of the
authors cited on these pages? We have neither the information nor the ability necessary to discuss particular cases. Nor
do we know what the ancient Fathers would have thought of
more recent teachings, since the time, let us say, of Isaac of
Nineveh. No general rule can fix the just measure for each
individual. This is precisely the role of discretion, the
appanage of the 'spirituals' who alone could properly exercise
the direction of souls. We do, however, know the principles
from which they drew their wisdom. Saint John Chrysostom
repeats them more than once in his letters to Olympias. First,
make sure that godly grief is not tainted by another, worldly
grief.

There is only one terrible thing, one real trial, and
that is sin. You have heard me say it again and
again. All the rest is a myth, call it what you will:
ambushes, insults, enmities, traps, calumnies,
exiles, sharpened swords, the ocean, or a world
war. Whatever may be these scourges, they are
things of passage. They concern only the mortal
body and have no way of hurting a soul which is
master of itself.[14]

Next, concerning sin itself, compunction must be carefully
maintained free from despair and discouragement.

You hear that one of the churches has gone down,
another is tossed about, and another overwhelmed
by furious waves. They are all afflicted with

incurable evils—one has a wolf instead of a shep-
herd, another a pirate instead of a pilot, another an
executioner instead of a physician. When you hear
of this you should, of course, suffer; it would not
do to hear these things without grief. But let your
suffering be controlled by limits. Even in the case
of our own faults, for which we will be held
accountable, it is not necessary or prudent—it is
even very harmful—to afflict ourselves excessively.
How much more in the case of others' faults is it
excessive and vain to lose courage? It is even
satanic, fatal to the soul.[15]

In support of this doctrine Chrysostom tells Olympias,
in all its detail, the story of the Corinthian guilty of
incest (1 Cor 5; 2 Cor 2:7). Elsewhere he returns to the same
theme:

Let no sinner despair, let no just man trust in his
virtue . . . . Saint Paul quickly raises up the fornicator who comes to repentance, lest he be ab-
sorbed in excessive sadness. Why then, O man, do
you let yourself be stricken by other accidents,
since even in sin, the only case where sadness can
help, excessiveness (ἀμετρία) does great harm?[16]

So true is this that, from the very start, compunction, if it is
to be authentic, must contain in germ the 'incomparable
sweetness' which will bloom later in the 'grace of tears'.[17]

As for this last stage, since the Spirit blows where it wills,
and with the strength that it wills, who would dare prescribe
laws? None are in fact to be found, with one exception: this
gift, like all other charisms, must be hidden for fear of vainglory. This in no way contradicts what was said above about
Saint Arsenius;[18] neither he nor any other desert Father
transgressed this rule of humility. The terms 'grace of tears'
or 'gift of tears' are foreign to the Sayings. The hermits wept
for their sins only because they wanted to, and they wanted
to because they believed it their duty. The first time that we

encounter the expression τὸ χάρισμα τῶν δακρύων is in the
*De virginitate* of Saint Athanasius.[19] The relations between
this shorter treatise and Evagrius' *Exhortatio ad virginem*[20]
require a closer examination than that given by van der Goltz,
who did not know the Greek text of Evagrius. In any case,
Evagrius himself gives an exact two-line summary of Athanasius' chapter seventeen: 'At night, beseech the Saviour with
tears, being sure that no-one sees you praying, and you will
find grace.'[21] In the *Chapters on Prayer* the recommendation
of humility becomes more insistent:

> If you should pour out fountains of tears in your
> prayer, do not lift yourself up inwardly. Your
> prayer has simply received help so that you can
> generously confess your sins, appeasing the Lord
> by your tears. Do not then turn the remedy for
> passions into passion, unless you wish to irritate
> further the giver of grace. Many have wept over
> their sins, but because they have forgotten the pur-
> pose of tears, they have been caught in madness
> and have gone astray.[22]

John the Solitary has already warned us against the temptation of attracting others' esteem through outward signs of
compunction. 'Let our *penthos* not be according to men',
writes someone under the name of Ephrem, 'nor be seen by
men, but let it be according to God, who sees the secrets of
the heart, so that by him we may be made blessed. Then we
will have a cheerful countenance . . . .'[23] Of course, this does
not mean that we should laugh; the sermon in question is
entitled, 'That we must not laugh or be frivolous, but rather
weep and mourn over ourselves'. Saint Theodore the Studite
formulates the 'rules of modesty' thus:

> Let us then keep our senses in safety, our looks
> cast down most of the time. Let the eye be
> restrained, not agitated and wandering here and
> there . . . . Our face should be neither sullen nor
> giddy, but somehow happily tempered and calm,

always bright with gravity and shining with tears of
compunction .... [24]

With these precisions in mind, we are ready to hear the
case for compunction's defense. It is first of all a question of
faith. 'How can we come to fear the judgements of God?'
someone asks Saint Basil.

> The expectation of some evil naturally produces
> fear in our souls. That is why we fear beasts as well
> as people set over us, when we are persuaded that
> they will do us some harm. Every man, then, who
> is convinced that God's threats are true, and who
> lives in expectation of their so terrible and fearful
> effects, will unquestionably fear his judgements. [25]

What holds for fear holds for compunction. Why do people
not have it? wondered Maximus the Confessor. He shows at
some length that the only reason is their lack of the fear of
God:

> The brother said, 'Father, why do I not have
> *catanyxis*?' The old man replied, 'Because the fear
> of God is not before our eyes. We have become
> the meeting place of all evils, and so it is that we
> scorn the terrible judgement of God as though it
> were a mere idea. For who would not be seized
> with compunction, hearing Moses speak of sinners
> in the name of God ....

There follow passages of the Old and New Testaments, all
introduced by the formulas 'Who would not be horrified ...
who would not tremble ... who would not shudder ... ? '
The prophets groaned over us, the apostle spoke in the same
way, Christ himself wept over Jerusalem, and we remain
cold? It is either because we have no faith or because we
pride ourselves on being in good standing with divine
justice.

> And so, woe to us! We have come to the farthest
> reaches of evil .... Are we not all gluttons? All
> lovers of pleasure? All ill-tempered, resentful,

inconstant in virtue, given to mocking, hotheaded, swollen with vanity, hypocrites, sly, jealous, unruly, lazy . . . ?

How then can we claim to have faith? At the very most, the faith which Saint James attributes to the demons themselves, dead faith, since it shows no vitality in works. Worse still, a hypocritical faith like that of the Pharisees: 'This people honors me with their lips, but their heart is far from me'.

> What Our Lord said against the Pharisees I take as directed to us, the Pharisees of today, we who have received such a great grace and who are worse than they. We too, do we not impose on others' shoulders burdens difficult to bear, without touching them with our fingers? We too, do we not perform our works to be seen by men? We too, do we not love the first places in assemblies and to be called by men, 'Rabbi, Rabbi?' And as for those who are not careful to pay us these honors, do we not wage deadly war against them . . . ? We build tombs for the martyrs and we decorate the monuments of the apostles, but we are like those who killed them. Who then would not weep over us, since we have such dispositions? Who would not deplore a captivity such as ours?[26]

That is why we have no compunction: we do not take seriously either the truths of faith or the sternness of morality.

If we really have faith, then there is only one other way to explain our shallowness: lack of intelligence. Saint Gregory of Nyssa has irrefutable reasoning to demonstrate this:

> If we have understood human mourning, let us go from the better known to the less, to discover what is the blessed mourning which is followed by consolation. If, then, in this world it is the privation of goods which produces mourning, it follows that no-one should moan over the loss

of an object of which he knows nothing. We must first know the good, know what it really is, and then reflect on human nature. That is how we will become capable of realizing blessed *penthos.* It is the same for those who live in shadows. One was born in darkness, while another was shut up in it through some misdeed after being accustomed to enjoy the light. Their common misfortune will not affect them in the same way. One, knowing what he has lost, will feel bitterly the loss of light. The other, having not the least idea of such a privilege, will continue to live without sorrow; because he is accustomed to the darkness, he will not feel deprived of any good. Then, the desire to enjoy the light will inspire in one every possible device to see again what the adversary has taken away from him. The other will grow old in darkness; he has never known anything better and will be satisfied with his present state. It is the same for the subject at hand. He who has learned to understand true good, and who has then reflected on the misery of human nature, will necessarily have a saddened soul. Because the present life does not give possession of that good, he will be in mourning. That is why I think that it is not sadness which the Word blesses, but knowledge of the good. This knowledge includes the feeling of sadness, because the good that we so desire is absent from life.[27]

This then is the teaching that I hear from Him who blesses *penthos:* let the soul lift its gaze toward the true good and let it not sink into the deceits of the present. It is not possible to live without tears if one considers things as they really are, just as it is impossible to feel sadness if we plunge into life's pleasures. We see the same thing in dumb animals.

Nature has given them a pitiful equipment (for
what could be more pitiful than lack of reason?),
but having no idea of their abasement, their life
too is passed in a certain kind of pleasure. The
horse puts on airs, the bull raises dust as he paws
the ground, the pig raises his bristles, puppies
frolic, calves jump about, and so it is that each of
the animals shows by certain signs the pleasure it
feels. And yet, if they had any idea of the privilege
of reason, their stupid and miserable life would not
be spent in pleasure. So it is with men: those who
have no knowledge of the goods of which our
nature has been deprived live in pleasure.[28]

Those, on the other hand, who approach their christian faith
rationally will have *penthos,* and by its means they will obtain consolations far superior to joys limited by ignorance.
With reasoning like this, the philosopher of the *Life of Moses*
emerges as the best apologist for the rustics of Egypt.

Even if a taste of Origenism lingers in these reflections of
Gregory of Nyssa, their forcefulness loses nothing thereby.
Although man is not a fallen god, in the sense that these
pages seem to assume, the loss of salvation through original
and personal sin remains as a fact to support Gregory's
reasoning. All too often, though, we are dazzled by words,
especially in questions of humility. We mistake humble
speech (ταπεινολογία) for humility (ταπεινοφροσύνη).[29] 'You
call yourself a sinner,' writes Saint Barsanuphius to a sus-
ceptible correspondent, 'but in practice you do not consider
yourself one . . . . You have called yourself a fool, but do not
mock yourself. Consider well, and you will find that you
do not believe it.'[30] It is frivolous to keep repeating 'Pray for
us, poor sinners,' and not to have compunction.

It might be, though, that we have a psychological excuse.
The sincerest thoughts do not always find feelings to match.
It is here that we are farthest away from the ancients. In
spite of their Platonism, their tendency to envision the body

as a mere dwelling or prison of the soul, they were less ambivalent than we. For them, the goal of asceticism was, precisely, to reduce the dualism of thought and feeling to the unity of the spiritual. This is because they had a very high concept of that 'nature' to which we return by pursuing perfection. The conflicts we all experience, even congratulating ourselves on them as an occasion of merit, appeared to the ancients as so many clear signs of imperfection. As long as they had not arrived at total peace through unification of instincts with will, of imagination with mind, then of will and mind with the divine will and truth, they persisted in blaming themselves and feeling themselves far from the health at which they aimed. 'At first the mind had as its master revelation through the spirit, but it turned away and became the pupil of the senses. Once again, through perfection in Christ, it will be favored with its first master.'[31]

This is the ultimate reason for the famous doctrine of *apatheia.* It is a travesty to speak of it as merely plagiarized from Stoicism. It certainly does not teach that feelings are to be destroyed. Rather, they are to be won back by the spirit, and to become its docile servants, instead of the undisciplined rebels which passion has made of them. We have already pointed out that spiritual sensitivity awakens to the extent that the exterior senses are mortified. This is the Ζωοποιὸς νέκρωσις of which Symeon the New Theologian speaks: a lifegiving death.[32] The school of the New Theologian held fast to the theory of the original unity in man's spirit, and of the split brought into the soul by sin. Symeon had read of this in the first book his spiritual father had given him, the hundred chapters of Diadochus:

> Even though the natural sense is one, as the power
> of sacred doctrine teaches, nevertheless it has been
> divided into two operations by the disobedience
> of Adam.
> The natural sense of the soul, as I have already
> said, is one (remember that the five senses differ

according to the body's needs). This is the teaching
of the Holy Spirit, the friend of men. Nevertheless
this one sense, because of our lapses into disobe-
dience, undergoes the same division as the movements of the soul. Thus, one part of this sense lets
itself be carried off by the passions, whence it
comes that we experience pleasure in the goods of
this life. The other part often prefers to follow the
rational and intellecutal movements of the soul,
whence it comes that our mind, at our better
moments, desires to run toward heavenly beauty. If
then we can make a firm habit of despising the
goods of the world, we will be able to join the
earthly appetite of the soul to its rational tendency. It is the communication of the Holy Spirit
which disposes us to this. If his divinity does not
effectively illumine the depths of the soul, we will
not be able to taste the good with an undivided
sense, that is with our whole and entire soul.[33]

It is in the light of these ideas that we should consider the
*commandment* to weep over the loss of salvation. Let us for
a moment abandon our psychological compartments and
suppose that we have overcome our dissident feelings. Now
we easily understand that emotions must follow the lead of
the mind. Each perception of the mind will have a corresponding feeling in the heart. The scale of emotions will
sound in unison with thoughts. Sorrow will be measured
against the value of the good that was lost. Now there is
nothing comparable to salvation. It is right, then, that
Evagrius should name as 'savagery' the hardness of 'the soul
which refuses to shed tears'; that Gregory of Nyssa should
speak of animal stupidity, Maximus the Confessor of lack of
faith. To force oneself to shed tears is simply to work at
re-establishing the broken balance between the higher and
lower senses. To excuse one's dryness solely on grounds
of temperament is to deceive oneself. We should accuse

ourselves, since it is our fault, for having lost our health or for not trying hard enough to regain it. 'If in the human composite God rules the mind, the mind of corporeal life, then it will remain in nature, but if it cuts itself off from nature, it will also escape the influence of the mind.'[34] It is this unnatural ambivalence which makes us resist compunction.

All well and good, you may say, for interior compunction—but tears? Except for Saint Dorotheos,[35] no-one seems to have asked himself the question: is there a *penthos* without tears? The Great Old Man, Saint Barsanuphius, avoided replying directly to this problem. Perhaps he thought it of little importance. What is in fact at issue? Whether a great sorrow, an intense regret which is both thought and felt, necessarily translates itself into tears. In other words, whether the soul's emotions necessarily communicate themselves to the organism. This is a physiological problem, far less important than the higher psychological question which preceded it. Still, the Fathers were concerned with this as well. It must be admitted that they never seem to have believed in the sincerity of an affliction which did not cause weeping. This was a conviction drawn from daily experience. They knew only too well that tears are a relief which sufferers are not likely to refuse, and to these men they preached moderation.[36] Nor were they unaware that some had made themselves sick, some even had died, from holding back tears in great distress.[37] These are exceptional cases which only show the more clearly how much the pangs of the heart affect the humors of the body. There is no known case of a man or woman who died of contrition over the loss of his soul, weeping for his sins. God has formed the human frame in such a way that, except in cases of congenital vice or a violent intervention of the will, a saddened heart causes that moisture which we call tears to rise to the eyes. Do you want to know how that happens? Saint Gregory of Nyssa will tell you that it is a mistake to speak of the heart in

this physiological process. When one's 'heart is wrenched',
it is really the opening of the stomach which contracts.

> Sorrow causes the subtle and invisible outlets of
> the pores to close. The interior organs are then
> compressed, which causes humid vapor to rise to
> the head and meninx and to accumulate in the
> cavities of the encephalon. Then, pushed out by
> the ducts at the base of the brain, it arrives at the
> eyes, where the contractile movement of the
> eyelids draws it out in the form of tears.[38]

The bishop of Nyssa must have thrashed out this question
with his brother from Caesarea. They are as good disciples of
Galen, in almost perfect agreement.[39]

Certain temperaments, however, find weeping difficult.
There are, says Saint Symeon the New Theologian, people
to whom 'even puncturing would not cause compunction'.[40]
After all that we have read, though, it must be admitted that
in the eyes of the Fathers such people are few. 'Tears are
like blood in the wounds of the soul,' as Saint Gregory of
Nyssa puts it.[41] It is natural that a wound should bleed, except among the bloodless. What can we say to them?

> I have often heard you say, as you do now (writes
> Saint Nilus to the deacon Agapetus), 'What shall
> I do? I want to weep and mourn over my sins, I
> even force myself, but not one tear comes to my
> eyes. I groan over this one fact with an anguished
> heart. If I see another weeping freely in Christ, I
> have to struggle against jealousy.' To this I reply
> that it is still worthwhile to desire tears. If you go
> to God with this desire, asking his pardon and
> salvation, you will be heard, as the psalm says,
> 'You will hear the desire of the meek' (Ps 10:17).
> And to the ruling faculty, the mind, it says, 'You
> have given him his heart's desire' (Ps 21:2). Who-
> ever desires a thing, be it good or bad, has already
> carried it out in his spirit . . . . Some people have a

physical constitution which is slow to furnish
tears. What must one do who desires tears? Do
this: Imagine your soul weeping as it keeps vigil, as
you have often seen it weeping in a dream. Weep
and shed tears before God in your intention, and
thus you can be purified from sins. It is to this that
the psalmist exhorts us: 'Pour out your heart before him' (Ps 62:8). Besides, I know some who did
not stop there, but by dint of faith and prayer
they changed the rock of their soul into a stream
of water (cf. Ps 114:8). Constantly pricking their
heart with the word of Christ and the remembrance of divine marvels, they have caused floods
of tears to spring up from within, through eyes of
stone. Still, if you yourself do not succeed in
obtaining a grace such as that, and if you see
another weeping in his prayers, glorify the Lord
for this, and say, "I thank you, my Lord God, for
having deprived me of this gift which purifies and
dissolves evil, and for having granted it to my
brother. Multiply your grace to him, O Master, to
the full, for my brother is my member, and when
one member is glorified, all the other members
rejoice with him' (cf. 1 Cor 12:26). If you feel this
way about your brother and dispose your spirit to
contentment concerning him, you will share with
him the charism he possesses, and a common
crown will fall to you both, provided that all is
done for Christ.[42]

The devil gets mixed up in this as well, profiting as he does
from the tendencies proper to each one's humors. 'Whence
comes warmth, cold, and hardness of heart?' someone asks
Saint Barsanuphius.

Concerning warmth and cold, it is clear that the
Lord has been named Fire, a fire which heats the
heart and the reins, making them burn. If this

is true, it follows that the devil is cold, and from him comes all coldness. If it were otherwise, how could the Lord say that then most men's love will grow cold (Mt 24:12)? What does the word 'then' mean, if not 'in the time of the adversary'? When we feel coldness, therefore, let us call upon God and he will come to warm our heart, causing it to arrive at perfect charity, not only toward himself but also toward our neighbor. Before his heat that coldness which is the enemy of all good will be banished. If the devil has dried up the source of tears in your eyes, you may be sure that he has irrigated the inferior organs. Only place the Lord in your dwelling, and he will dry up that humidity, purifying the source of tears and causing the stream of spiritual waters to flow. Whoever wishes to arrive at the fear of God will do so through patience, as it is written, 'I waited patiently for the Lord; he inclined to me and heard my cry'. And then what? 'He drew me up from the desolate pit, out of the miry bog' (Ps 40:1,2). To this pit corresponds also our hardness of heart. Acquire therefore what you desire, and you will be saved in the Lord.[43]

Is it necessary to add that, in the times of the Fathers, people in mourning indulged in louder shows of grief than they do today? The fact is certain; one need look no further than the text of Saint John Chrysostom, cited above, on the kings who do not refuse to undergo the law of mourning.[44] The institution of professional mourners is based on the idea that there are at least some people whose talent it is to shed tears at will. Has human psychology taken significant steps forward in this matter? The question is open to speculation, but does not lend itself to conclusions unfavorable to *penthos*. There are still people today who can weep when they feel like it, and if professional mourners have disappeared, this is probably because people in mourning no longer feel the need of their services. So much for that subject. It was raised only to dispose of the possible objection that we had not thought of it.

Finally, the 'gift of tears' does pose a problem of mysticism. Here again we will be brief, and for several reasons. First, for lack of competence; then, because the Fathers, even though they wrote enough about tears to fill a book ten times the size of this one, seem to have forgotten about this last chapter, at least until Isaac of Nineveh. Lastly, because the mystic element in weeping raises the more general question of mysticism itself. At least this much is special to our topic: is it true, as the school of the New Theologian claims, that 'tears of compunction' are the clearest possible sign of 'grace'?[45] This is for theorists to solve. We will have done our job if we can show that the *penthos* preached by the Fathers is not essentially mystical, but that it springs initially from *ascesis*. In fact, the point appears to be already proved. Weeping for our sins is a duty. This is the realm of the commandments, of *praxis*. How amazed the Fathers would have been if someone had said to them, 'I am waiting for the charism of tears to get me started on *penthos*, on "mourning" for lost salvation!' Some, indeed, among those most favorable to mysticism have trenchant statements which exclude all confusion. But beware of translations! The fourth Instruction of Saint Ammonas begins with this sentence, from the translation of F. Nau: 'Beloved, let us strengthen ourselves in tears before God ....' In reality, the text should read, 'My dear brothers, let us do everything possible, let us use all our strength to shed tears before God. Perhaps his charity will send us a power to keep us until we have conquered ... ' .[46] Weeping first—that is a must. Mysticism afterwards, if it is God's will. Saint John Climacus, precisely at the end of his Seventh Degree, where '*penthos* the cause of joy' begins to take on a mystical aspect unknown until then, feels the need for making some things

clear. He speaks unusually sharply, as if in opposition to the
partisans of contrary and erroneous opinions:

> You there! We will not have to answer, at the
> moment of the soul's departure, for not having
> been wonderworkers or theologians, nor for not
> having become contemplatives, but we must
> unavoidably render an account to God for not
> having practiced *penthos* without interruption.[47]

Whether mystical or not (the question is not really important), compunction for John Climacus, in any of the forms
in which he describes it, is always within our reach.

Isaac of Nineveh himself—and it is not my business here
to reconcile all his sayings—proves the necessity of perpetual
compunction with an argument which contains nothing
specifically mystical.

> All just men have left this world in tears. If the
> saints wept and always had their mouth full of
> tears . . . who would not weep? . . . If those who
> were victorious wept here below, how is it that
> one who is full of ulcers would cease weeping? A
> father, certainly, who has before him the body of
> a beloved child, does not need to be taught which
> thoughts will arouse tears in him. Your soul lies
> before you, dead through sin, and it is worth more
> to you than the whole world. If we go into solitude,
> we will thus be able to render tears perpetual. Let
> us then ask insistently that Our Lord give them to
> us. If we receive this gift, more excellent than any
> other, we will attain to purity through tears. And
> if we do reach it, that purity will not be taken
> away from us again until our departure from
> this world.[48]

This *a fortiori* would make no sense if the Ninevite thought
of *penthos,* even continual *penthos,* as a charism reserved for
the perfect. Like every virtue, it is a grace.

Symeon the New Theologian's thirty-second sermon sets

out to justify a saying of his spiritual father, 'Brother, without tears you will never receive communion'.[49] The translator Pontanus protests, albeit gently, against the exaggerated importance given to material tears.[50] The Studite's contemporaries doubted in fact whether such compunction were possible.

> The many hearers, not only lay people but also famous monks, known for their virtue, were astonished at these words. They looked at each other and said, as though smiling, in a single voice, 'Well, then, we will never receive communion, we will all remain without communion'.[51]

Throughout his long apology, the New Theologian defends his venerated father with a stream of arguments, all showing that lack of compunction stems only from laxity of life.

> Whence comes it, you say, that one is hard, another soft toward compunction? Listen: from resolution and will, good in one, bad in another; from works, signs in one of divine love, signs of the opposite in another.

Thus Symeon recounts, in vehement tones, the means to be taken for acquiring and keeping *penthos*. Pontanus opposes him with Durandus, Saint Thomas, and Cassian who, as we have seen, does not follow his master Evagrius on this point. Symeon is in the tradition of his Eastern Church; his sermon is laden with allusions, some of them almost textual, to the writings of the Fathers. Pontanus shows a better sense of context in his reference to Isaac and Homily 107 of Antiochus. With these, and many others, the great Byzantine mystic considers compunction as primarily a part of *ascesis*.

Of course he may have exaggerated; that is another question, which belongs in its turn to the more general question of penitential practices. If I may add a thought for today's Christians, I would recommend that they take careful note of this doctrine, and first thank the Lord all the more for the *sacrament* of penance, but then beware lest they think themselves dispensed from the *virtue* of repentance, essential both to salvation and perfection. Eastern spirituality, like all christian spirituality, has very high ambitions—the joy of the resurrection, deification. Even as it aims thus high, it warns the faithful not to deceive themselves into thinking that they have actually done all that they have thought, read, or written. What it sets before them is not a speculation to be understood, but a life to be lived ever more and more intensely. The law of this progress, so necessary to life, was expressed by Origen in three words borrowed from philosophy and transposed to a higher plane: πρᾶξις θεωρίας ἀνάβασις (practice is the ascent to contemplation).[52] Generations will pass along this law; Nicephoras the Monk will repeat it long centuries after Gregory the Theologian.[53] Gregory adds that this is where Christians can be distinguished from philosophers. They must either pass through *ascesis* or remain at the 'mere knowledge' of the pagans. What else is this than the very law of the Gospel? *Per crucem ad lucem* says a Latin equivalent to Origen's formula. In our context it would be: through mourning to happiness.

The last word, as in all the evangelical beatitudes, is saved for joy. God did not create us for weeping, but *'ut haberet in quem collocaret sua beneficia'*—that he might have someone in whom to place his great gifts.[54] This fundamental truth of Christianity was never forgotten by the 'old men'.

> Abba Longinus said, 'Fasting humiliates the body; vigils purify the spirit; silence brings *penthos; penthos* baptizes a man and frees him from sin'. Now Abba Longinus had great compunction in his prayer and psalmody. His disciple therefore said to him once, 'Abba, is that the spiritual canon, that the monk weep always in the liturgy?' The old man answered, 'Yes, my child, such is the rule which the Lord wishes of us *now*. In the beginning God did not make man for sorrowing (ἵνα πενθῇ), but

so that he might have joy and gladness, thus
glorifying him in purity and sinlessness like the
angels. But when man fell into sin, he needed
tears, and so it has been ever since. On the other
hand, where there is no sin, there is no further
need for tears'.[55]

How wrong it would be to speak of 'christian pessimism'
when talking of those who alone are not without hope, and
still worse to speak of the unchristian pessimism of those
whose hope has entered into the life of their emotions.
Blinder yet are those who tax the Fathers with soft senti-
mentality. The slogan 'live dangerously' acquires its full
meaning only when we open our eyes to the risks of
eternity. The heroes of *penthos* had quite another moving
force in their enthusiasm (the exact word here) for supernatural horizons, a force strong enough to make them im-
pervious to the 'myths' of earthly perils. Optimism and
realism, enthusiasm and discretion, strength of character and
sweetness, ambition and humility, passion for God and sacrifice of self, charity of one's neighbor and lack of self-seek-
ing; above all, the logic of faith, a perfect sincerity and
rigorous consistency—that is what close study has shown us
of their psychology. We have the right as well as the duty to
be proud of such ancestors.

Above all, let us not feel sorry for them. They called
themselves happy, and surely they were the best judges of
that. Never once have we encountered the word 'unhappy'
applied to those who weep. 'The ineffable sweetness of tears'
must indeed correspond with the truth, since they speak of
it even among themselves. 'I wish I could always weep like
this.' There is no denying that the divine ambition urging
them on, and their conviction of the obligation and possibility of gaining their objective, all cast on their expressions a
very special type of seriousness. To the superficial glance
this seriousness may seem to resemble the sadness which
they abhor, but in fact this gravity is filled with happiness

as it grows ever deeper. Saint Arsenius, the Sayings assure us, had an angelic appearance.[56] For those in the Eastern Church, at least as much as for Saint Francis de Sales, 'un sainte triste est un triste saint' (A sad saint is a sorry saint). The infallible sign of perfection is unshakeable peace. Do not tears of joy betray the most exquisite happiness? That is why they are so rare in human relations. For those who are close to God, they last forever.

We have seen Saint Anthony weeping and lamenting over another's sin.[57] Not to him would Saint John Chrysostom have said, 'I do not ask you to shed tears for others; I would like it, but it is too high for you'.[58] Saint Athanasius also tells us that Anthony groaned every day over himself.[59] Despite this, or rather, because of it,

> his countenance had a great and wonderful grace. This gift he also had from the Saviour. For if he were present in a great company of monks, and anyone who did not know him previously wished to see him, unhesitatingly coming forward he passed by the rest and hurried to Anthony, as though attracted by his appearance. Yet neither in height nor in breadth was he conspicuous above others, but in the serenity of his manner and the purity of his soul. For as his soul was free from disturbances, his outward appearance was calm; so from the joy of his soul he possessed a cheerful countenance, and from his bodily movements could be perceived the condition of his soul . . . . Thus Anthony was recognized: he was never disturbed, his soul was at peace; he was never downcast, for his mind was joyous.[60]

'Where is Abba Anthony?' someone asked. 'He is in the place where God is.'[61] 'The place of God, that is peace.'[62]

*Beata pacis visio!*

Anthony the Great is the father of all the monks of the East and of the West.

# NOTES

## TRANSLATOR'S PREFACE

1.  I speak only of wholesale movements, trends. What the Holy Spirit does in calling specific religious groups or individuals to sanctity is not to be denied. Desert monasticism has in fact revived in Egypt. [See, for example, *Contemporary Monasticism* (Oxford: SLG Press, 1981) pp 11-22.] As for tears, see the interesting story of the actress Eve LaVallière as told by Raïssa Maritain in *Adventures in Grace*. After her conversion, LaVallière's eyes were constantly irritated from perpetual weeping. Today this seems exceptional. Once, Father Hausherr tells us, it was the rule.

## INTRODUCTION

1.  N. Arseniev, *Ducha Pravoslavia* (Novy Sad, 1927) p. 5.
2.  Ward, p. 6.
3.  Evagrius, letter 58. Frankenberg, p. 608.

## CHAPTER I

1.  E. Boisacq, *Dictionnaire étymologique de la langue grecque* (Heidelberg, 1916).
2.  At the word πένθος Suidas, however, notes this meaning: '... and sacred *penthos* such as is in Lebanon for Adonis and in Byblos'. The same remark occurs at Ἄδωνις. For sacred mourning over Adonis, see Lucian *De Dea Syra*, 6.
3.  Evagrius, *Praktikos* II, 95; PG 140: An English translation by J. E. Bamberger *Evagrius Ponticus: Praktikos and Chapters on Prayer*, Cistercian Studies Series, Nbr 4 (1972) may be consulted.
4.  *In epistolam ad Philemon hom.* 3, n. 3; PG 62:202 f.
5.  Gregory Nazianzen, *In laudem Caesarii* 15; PG 35:755 f.
6.  VS III; PL 73:1029 ff.
7.  Alph. Euprepios 2; Ward, pp. 52 f.

8. Barsanuphius, letter 682, p. 327. See Pseudo-Ephrem, *De compunctione animi* (Roman edition) I:31 f.

9. Compare the 25 kinds of λύπη according to Andronicos. See H.F.A. von Arnim, *Stoicorum veterum fragmenta* (Leipzig, 1923) 3:100. None of these kinds of sadness, except for compassion, appears in the ascetic literature.

10. Evagrius, *Ad Monachos* 56; *De oratione* 12, 5; Bamberger, 56-7.

11. Evagrius, *Antirrheticon,* 'Accedia', 38; Frankenberg, p. 526.

12. P.A. de Lagarde, ed., *Constitutiones Apostolorum* (Reprint: Osnabruck, 1966) p. 207.

13. See R.H. Connolly, *Didascalia Apostolorum* (Oxford, 1929) pp. 190, 192.

CHAPTER II

1. Isidore of Pelusium discusses this word in *Epist.* 4.101; PG 78:1165C-1169A, and cites several examples with a favorable sense.

2. At Ps 29:13 occurs the verb κατανυγῶ not the substantive.

3. *In epistolam ad Romanos* 19.1; PG 60:584.

4. Alph. Timothy 1, Ward, p. 199.

5. VS III.17; PL 73: 862D.

6. Alph. Euprepios 7; Ward, p. 53.

7. PE III.29, p. 81.

8. Dorotheos, *Doctr.* XXI, Interrogation 2, in Barsanuphius, *Epist.* 282, p. 153.

9. Some have understood these 'catanyctics' in the sense of 'nocturns'. Balthasar Corder corrects them in his translation of Saint Dorotheos (Prague, 1726), p. 309, note to *Institutio* XX: 'Antiquus interpres vertit *nocturnos sermones,* cum vertere debuisset *sermones compunctorios,* sive ad compungendum aptos. Intelligit enim dicta Patrum, exquisitas sententias, quae compunctionem, sive pium animi sensum commovere solent, ἀπὸ τοῦ κατανύττεσθαι compungi. Nam ἀπὸ τῆς νυκτός non nisi in tenebris haurire potuit *interpres* sus istos nocturnos sermones.'

CHAPTER III

1. *Paedagogos* 2.57.56; ed. Stählin 1:191.

2. *Laws* 5.

3. *Paed.,* p. 194.
4. *Stromata* 4.5.26; ed. Stählin 2:259.
5. *Ibid.* 4.6.37; p. 265.
6. *In Ieremiam* 3.49; ed. Stählin 3:267.
7. Jer 20:7. PG 13:513 B-D.
8. *In Lucam, hom.* 18; PG 13:1897BC.
9. *In Ieremiam* 16.10. Here Origen depends on Philo. Cf. W. Völker, *Fortschritt und Vollendung bei Philo von Alexandrien* (Leipzig, 1938) 110 f.
10. *In Ps. 38, hom.* 2.7.
11. *In Thren.,* Fragment 31, ed. Klostermann, p. 250.
12. *In Ieremiam* 19.3.
13. W. Völker, *Das Vollkommenheitsideal des Origenes* (Tübingen, 1931), pp. 33 ff., 37 ff., 158 f.
14. *Ibid.,* p. 159, note 2.
15. *Letter* 3.11.
16. PG 117: 309-314.
17. PG 156:576.
18. Posthumous edition (Venice, 1816).
19. Ἐπιτομὴ ἐκ τῶν προφητανακτοδαβιτικῶν ψαλμῶν. . . (Constantinople, 1799).
20. Cf. J. de Guibert, 'La componction du coeur,' in *Revue d'Ascétique et de Mystique* 15 (1934) 229.
21. (Moscow, 1820; second edition, 1824).


CHAPTER IV

1. *Centuries* 1.70, 71; PG 120:884 B.
2. *Neon Eclogion* (Constantinople, 1863), p. 213, col. 2.
3. *De beatitudine* 3; PG 44:1224 A.
4. *Alph. Poemen* 12, 99; Ward, pp. 142, 152.
5. *Alph. Moses, instr.* 7; Ward, p. 120. Hausherr's 'Master' is 'the Lord' in Ward's translation.
6. Ward, p. 119 f.
7. *Alph. Sisoes* 20, 36; Ward, pp. 182, 184.
8. *Ad Nicolaum praecepta salutaria;* PG 65:1028-1053.
9. *Ibid.,* 2.
10. *De his qui putant se ex operibus iustificari* 205 ff; PG 65:961.
11. Mark uses this word rarely. See, however, *Praecepta Salutaria* 11; PG 65:1045 D.
12. *De Paenitentia* 11; PG 65:981 A.

13.   *De his* 139; cf. 140.

14.   Mark the Hermit is a difficult author, as Photius *(Bibliotheca Cod. CC)* had already noted, Combefis, Bellarmine and others suspect him of errors (cf. PG 65:896). At the very passage that we have just cited is adjoined the marginal note, 'Caute legas'. I feel that only his vocabulary goes astray. He deserves a careful study.

15.   Basil has left no specific discourse on virginity. The treatise under this title, which is attributed to him, is by Basil of Ancyra, and the text cited by Nicodemus is not a part of it.

16.   On penance: *Scala* degree 5; On penthos: degree 7.

17.   Book 5.3, Book 7.22-24; PL 73:860-864.

18.   PL 73:1645D.

19.   Homily 51; PG 132:913.

20.   Τοῦ ὁσίου Πατρὸς ἡμῶν Ἡσαΐου λόγοι κθ', ed. Augustinos (Jerusalem, 1911), p. 60.

21.   *De paenitentia* 10; PG 65:980.

22.   PG 31.881 B.

23.   *Praktikos* 1.40; PG 40:1232 B; *ibid.,* 22; col. 1228; Bamberger, *Praktikos* 33, p. 25.

24.   *De oratione* 5; PG 79:1168D; *ibid.,* 6; Bamberger, p. 56.

25.   Evagrius, *Praktikos* 1.40; Bamberger, CS 4:34.

26.   OCP 5, p. 40.

27.   VS 5.3.10; PL 73:862A (Cf. 5.3.11). Alph. Poemen 26; Ward, p. 143.

28.   Alph. Euprepios 6; Ward, p. 53.

29.   VS 5.3.24.

30.   *Ibid.*

CHAPTER V

1.   *De compunctione* 1.10; PG 47:409F.

2.   PG 46:829 D.

3.   *Sermones Exegetici, In Is 26.10:* 'Tollatur peccator et non videat gloriam'. Ephrem 2:346 f.

4.   *Oratio* 16.13-14; PG 35:952B.

5.   *Oratio* 4, *Contra Iulianum* 1; PG 35:593C.

6.   *Carminum Liber* 2.46.27-30; PG 37:1379 f.

7.   *Ibid.* 2.51.12; col. 1395.

8.   *Confession Orthodoxe.* Latin text ed. A. Malvy and M. Viller (Paris–Rome, 1927) 85 f.

9.   PE 2.32, p. 103; arm. 1, p. 546.

10. Alph. Arsenius 4, 6; Ward, p. 8.
11. VS 3.1; PL 73:860 C. Cf. Ward, p. 16.
12. Alph. Arsenius 40; Ward, p. 15.
13. *Vie de Syméon,* 55; p. 72.
14. PE 2.32, p. 103; Arm. 1, p. 547.
15. PE 1.5, p. 18; Arm. 1, p. 522 f.
16. PE 3.9, p. 22-27.
17. Ephrem 1:32 D.
18. The Beatitudes are a new decalogue. *Philocalia* 2, pp. 13-16.
19. *Ad pop. Antioch.* 15.1; PG 49:154.
20. Alph. Poemen 122; Ward, p. 155.
21. Karl Heussi, *Der Ursprung des Mönchtums* (Tübingen, 1936) 220.
22. PG 79:1249 C. In PE 1.45, p. 161 this saying is attributed to Evagrius.
23. Cf. Is 6.5. PE 1.45, p. 142. Alp. Matoes 2. Ward, p. 121.
24. *Life of Saint Dositheus,* ed. P.M. Brun, *Orientalia Christiana* 26:109 ff. [Summarized at length in *Dorotheos of Gaza: Discourses and Sayings,* CS 33 (1977) 37-44—ed.]
25. PE 4.13, p. 60; Arm. 2, p. 339.
26. PE 1.45, p. 166; Arm. 2, p. 282.
27. Alph. Macarius 37; Ward, p. 115.
28. *First Greek Life* 1.106, 107, 114; Halkin, 107, 114; Veilleux, CS 45:371-2, 378-9.
29. Cf. Plutarch *De Stoicorum repugnantiis* 7.
30. ἀντακολουγυθῶσιν is a technical term of the Stoics.
31. Evagrius *Gnostikos* 109; Greek text in OCP 5:232.
32. Other comparisons are given here. See Nilus, *De oratione* 1.
33. Ephrem 1:61. This text is certainly not genuine for the very reason that this Stoic theory appears in it, and also because it speaks of Stylites. It seems to me of Syriac origin, nevertheless, at the time of Heraclius at the latest.
34. *Vitae Patrum* 7.38; PL 73:1055C.
35. Alph. Poemen 119; Ward, p. 155.
36. PE 2.32, p. 102.
37. *Short Rules* 31.
38. Homily 9; PG 31. 257 D.
39. *In Epist. ad Phil.* 3.4; PG 62:203.
40. E. Auvray, ed., *Petite Catéchèse* (Paris, 1891) p. 25.
41. Alph. Anthony 14; Ward, p. 3.
42. Alph. Poemen 114, 166; Ward, p. 154, 159.
43. Alph. Macarius 32, 25; Ward, p. 113, 112.

44. Alph. Anthony 23; Ward, p. 10.
45. Alph. John the Dwarf 14; Ward, p. 75.
46. Alph. Elias 2, 8; Ward, p. 60 f.
47. Cf. Clement of Rome, *Epistle to the Corinthians* 2.6, tr. James A. Kleist (Westminster, Md., 1946) p. 10: 'Over the failings of your neighbors you mourned; their shortcomings you judged to be your own'.
48. *First Greek Life* 100; Halkin, p. 67; Veilleux, CS 45:367.
49. *Ibid.*, 131; Halkin, p. 83; CS 46:390-1.
50. *Ibid.*, 146; Halkin, pp. 92f; CS 45:403-4.
51. Cf. Alph. Sisoes 13; Ward, p. 180, and note 46 in J.-B. Cotelier, 1; *ad loc.*
52. VS 7.41.2; PL 73:1056 D.
53. *Life of Saint Syncletica* 60; Cotelier, 1:240.
54. John Climacus, *Scale;* PG 88:1148 C.
55. Mark the Hermit, *De paenitentia* 11. Cf. 'L'erreur fondamentale et la logique du messalianisme', OCP 1:354 ff.
56. Alph. Sisoes 14; Ward, p. 180.
57. VS 7.13.7; PL 73:1036 D.
58. Is this by Paul Helladicos? See the edition of Papadopoulo-Kerameus, *Pravosl. Palest. Sbornik* 11.2:15.
59. *First Greek Life*, 7; Halkin, p. 5; CS 45:302.
60. Alph. Tithoes 6; Ward, p. 198.
61. Alph. John the Dwarf 23; Ward, p. 77: 'Forgive me, Abba, for I have not yet made a beginning'.
62. Alph. Macarius 2, 31; Ward, pp. 106, 113.
63. PE 3.26, p. 72 b.
64. Alph. Arsenius 27; Ward, p. 11.
65. Alph. Poemen 144; Ward, p. 157.
66. Alph. Anthony 32; Ward, p. 6. Cf. 1 John 4:18.
67. Alph. Amoun of Nitria 1; Ward, p. 27.
68. *Scale* 29; PG 88:1148D.
69. *Doctrina* 4.2; PG 88:1660 B; CS 33:110.
70. PE 3.36-42, p. 106-128.
71. PE 4.4, p. 12-19.
72. The two already cited (nn. 66, 67) and Alph. Anthony 28; Ward, p. 6. A fourth, somewhat astonishing in this place, is VS 5.11, n. 52.
73. *Vie de Syméon*, Introduction, pp. xxxi, xlviii.
74. See the index of the volume just cited, at δάκρυα.
75. *Life* 5.
76. Cf. Bedjan, p. 430; Wensinck, p. 288.

## CHAPTER VI

1.  *Oratio* 19, 'Ad Iulianum tributorum exaequatorem' 7; PG 35: 1049C.
2.  Cf. *Oratio* 14.5, 43.60; PG 35:864, PG 36:573.
3.  *De virginitate* 17; PG 28:272C.
4.  Nilus, *De oratione* 7,8.
5.  *Short Rules* 16.
6.  Ephrem, *Sermo Asceticus,* 1:60.
7.  R. Raabe, *Petrus der Iberer* (1895), p. 31 of the Syriac text.
8.  VII.7.
9.  PG 31: 304-328.
10. n. 2: 308C.
11. *The Cathedral of Homilies of Severus of Antioch,* ed. Rubens Duval, PO 4:23-44.
12. *Ibid.,* p. 35.
13. *Ibid.,* p. 34.
14. *Ibid.,* pp. 37, 42.
15. *Ibid.,* p. 54. Cf. p. 60.
16. *Homilia de terrae motu;* PG 50:713.
17. PE 2.2, p. 14.
18. Alph. Arsenius 21; Ward, p. 10.
19. Alph. Sisoes 34; Ward, p. 184.
20. A. Boon, *Pachomiana Latina* (Louvain, 1932) p. 59; CS 46: 173 translated from the Coptic text, has 'He shall not be crushed in tribulation. He shall fear not death but God'.
21. Alph. Theodore of Pherme 24; Ward, p. 66.
22. Alph. Or 12; Ward, p. 207.
23. PE 3.2, p. 14.
24. Alph. Moses, Instructions 7, 6; Ward, p. 120.
25. Alph. Pambo 4; Ward, p. 165.
26. *First Greek Life* 105; Halkin, p. 126; CS 45:369.
27. Alph. Poemen 17; Ward, 142.
28. Alph. Anthony 16; Ward, p. 3.
29. Ephrem 1:254 F: 'Quod non oporteat ridere et extolli, sed plangere potius et nos ipsos deflere.'
30. n. 76; Halkin, p. 51; CS 45:349.
31. Ephrem 1:31 E: *De compunctione animi.*
32. Alph. Dioscoros 2; Ward, p. 46.
33. *Life* 62; Halkin, p. 42; CS 45:340-1.
34. *Orsiesii liber* 42; Boon, *Pachomiana Latina,* p. 136; CS 47: 201.

35.  *Paralipomena Pachomiana* 2-4; Halkin, p. 127; Veilleux, *Pachomian Koinonia* II, CS 46:21-5.
36.  *Callinici de Vita S. Hypatii Liber*, ediderunt seminarii Bonnensis sodales (Leipzig, 1895) 73.
37.  Cf. above, p. 54.
38.  PE 2.32, p. 103, col. 2.
39.  Evagrius, *Centuries* 6.52.
40.  Dorotheos, *Institutio* 11; PG 88:1740 B; CS 33:175-8.
41.  A. Boon, *Pachomiana Latina*, 'Sancti Pachomii Praecepta,'; CS 46:151, 166.
42.  Alph. Evagrius 1; Ward, p. 54. *Vitae Patrum* 3.3.
43.  Alph. Arsenius 41; Ward, p. 16.
44.  *De beatitudine* 3; PG 44:1232.
45.  PE 2.32, p. 102.
46.  *Sermo Compunctorius*, Ephrem 1:28-40.
47.  Alph. Macarius 38; Ward, p. 115.
48.  PE 1.5, p. 18. Arm. 1, p. 543 ff.
49.  PE 1.5, p. 18. Arm. 1, p. 527.
50.  Alph. Theophilus the Archbishop 5; Ward, p. 70.
51.  Saint Theodore the Studite, *Catechesis* 83, ed. Papadopoulo–Kerameus (St Petersburg, 1904) p. 586. See the translation in *Orientalia Christiana* 6.22:17 ff.
52.  Cf. *ibid.*, pp. 165, 218.
53.  *First Greek Life* 91; Halkin, p. 61; CS 45:359.
54.  *Paralipomena* 3; Halkin, p. 126; CS 46:22-3.
55.  Alph. Silvanus 10 (cf. 3, 5, 12); Ward, p. 188 (186-8).
56.  Alph. Silvanus 2; Ward, p. 186.
57.  Alph. Dioscoros 3; Ward, p. 46.
58.  PG 65:161 ff., and note 12.
59.  Heussi, *Der Ursprung des Mönchtums*, p. 193 f.
60.  *In epist. ad Phil.* 3.4; PG 62:204.
61.  Alph. Anthony 38; Ward, p. 7.
62.  Barsanuphius, letter 417, p. 165.
63.  PE 1.21, p. 65. Arm. 2, p. 160.
64.  I. Herwegen, *Väterspruch und Mönchsregel* (Münster in W., 1937).
65.  *Ursprung des Mönchtums*, p. 164 f.
66.  Barsanuphius, letter 795, p. 460 ff (460 is a misprint for 360).
67.  Letter 360, p. 183.
68.  Letter 701, p. 335.
69.  *Ibid.*
70.  PE 2.32, p. 104.

71. Letter 65, p. 86. See the titles of letters 65 and 66.
72. Alph. Anthony 13; Ward, p. 3.
73. VS 7.38.1, and 'Appendix ad Vitas Patrum. Aegyptiorum Patrum Sententiae', 33; PL 74:387 C.
74. See above, pp. 38-9.
75. Diadochus of Photice, *Diadochi De perfectione spirituali capita centum,* ed. J.E. Weis–Liebersdorf (Leipzig, 1912) p. 90. [An English translation has appeared in *The Philocalia. The Complete Text,* I (London: Faber & Faber, 1980).]
76. PE 2.32, p. 102. Arm. 1, p. 523, recension 2.
77. Barsanuphius, letter 255, p. 140.
78. PE 2.32, p. 105.
79. Codex Berol. Phill. 1624, fol. 212a. See W. Bousset, *Apophthegmata* (Tübingen, 1923) 117.
80. PE 4.1, p. 8.
81. Alph. Arsenius 1, 2, 13; Ward, pp. 8-9.
82. Alph. Arsenius 2, 7; Ward, p. 8.
83. PE 1.13, p. 41. Arm. 2, p. 180.
84. PE 4.37, p. 125. Arm. *ubi supra.*
85. PE 2.32, p. 103. The word 'difference' is obtained by reading διαφορᾶς instead of διαφδορᾶς.
86. Barsanuphius, letter 458, p. 227.
87. See Hausherr, 'Méthode d'oraison hésychaste', *Orientalia Christiana* 9.36:169.
88. Bedjan, p. 130.
89. Alph. Moses 6; Ward, p. 118.
90. Alph. Macarius 27; Ward, p. 112.
91. *Ibid.* 41, p. 116.
92. Alph. Anthony 10; Ward, p. 2. See Life of Anthony 85.
93. Alph. Paphnutius 5; Ward, p. 170.
94. Inok Teofan in the Serbian periodical *Duhovna Straza* 8.4 (1935) 203-206.
95. PE 2.47, p. 144.
96. Alph. Tithoes 2; Ward, p. 198 translates *xeniteia* as 'pilgrimage'.
97. VS 5.4.27; PL 73:868 C.
98. Alph. Poemen 140; Ward, p. 157. See Alph. John the Dwarf 32; Ward, p. 78: 'Since you came here, you have driven God away from me.'
99. *Collationes* 9.30.
100. It is as though Evagrius were two men: the disciple of Saints Basil and Macarius, and the philosopher. In any synthesis of his

doctrine one ought not to forget the first without, however, drawing such false conclusions as that, when he turned to Origen, he totally set aside the preacher and director of souls.

101. *Paraeneticus,* Frankenberg, p. 560.

102. *Oratio* 17, 21.

103. For Origen, see Völker, *Das Vollkommenheitsideal,* p. 27; for Saint Athanasius or Saint Anthony, see the Life of Anthony 20.

104. *Antirrheticos,* 'Accedia', 10.

105. *Ibid.,* 'Accedia', 19.

106. Frankenberg, p. 556; see the French translation by Hausherr, 'Le Traité de l'Oraison d'Évagre le Pontique', *Revue d'Ascétique et de Mystique* 15 (Toulouse, 1934) 16.

107. Barsanuphius, letter 459, p. 227.

108. See above, p. 54.

109. Short Rules 90.

110. PE 2.32, p. 101.

111. *Neon Eclogion* (Constantinople, 1863) p. 216-217.

112. *Ibid.,* p. 255.

113. *Great Catechesis,* ed. Papadopoulo–Kerameus, p. 118, 892.

114. PE 2.32, p. 101.

115. See above, p. 3-4.

116. See the *Antirrheticos* of Evagrius, at the chapters on sadness and *accedia.*

117. PE, see above, note 114.


CHAPTER VII

1. *Peri Archon* 1.8; ed. Koetschau, p. 104.

2. *Scale* 13; PG 88:932.

3. See Philo, *Vita Moysis* 1.49.

4. *Centuries* 5.41.

5. *Centuries* 4.85.

6. *Praktikos* 2.62; CS 4:33.

7. *Centuries* 1.37.

8. Hausherr, 'Le Traité', p. 99.

9. See above, pp. 4-5.

10. Evagrius, *Antirrheticos,* 'Accedia', 38; Frankenberg, p. 527.

11. *Ibid.,* 'Gastrimargia', 24; p. 477.

12. PE 2.32, p. 104.

13. Evagrius, *Praktikos* 30; CS 4:24.

14. Evagrius, *letter* 51; Frankenberg, p. 598.

15. Alph. Xanthias 3; Ward, p. 134.
16. Barsanuphius, letter 459, p. 228; letter 155, p. 78.
17. Barsanuphius, letter 255, p. 140.
18. Alph. Sarah 5; Ward, p. 193. Barsanuphius is citing from memory.
19. Barsanuphius, letter 236, p. 127.
20. Who will give us a better edition than that of Nicodemus, which is almost impossible to find?
21. Origen, *Comm. in Matth.* 67; ed. Klostermann, p. 15, 1. 27 f.
22. I have forgotten which Greek author claims that Parisians got their name because of their 'parrhesia'. In any case, he does not say what sort of 'parrhesia' he means.
23. See for example the Life of Saint Euthymius. Cotelier, 2:256.
24. See Saint Dorotheos, *Doctrina* 4.5, 6; PG 88:1665; CS 33:114.
25. *De perfectione spiritus* 81.
26. PG 56:124.
27. PG 34:1090.
28. Alph. Agaton 1; Ward, p. 17.
29. Ephrem 1:254. The citation of Agathon is enough proof that this 'Sermo de non ridendo' is not by Saint Ephrem.
30. PE 2.34, 107.
31. A. Mai. *Nova Patrum Bibliotheca* (Rome, 1852 ff.) 8:196.
32. Lk 6:20-26.
33. *In laudem sancti Basilii* 67; PG 36:493 ff., 585.
34. *Short Rules* 31; PG 31:1104 B.
35. *Long Rules* 17; PG 31:961 f.
36. Cf. *Short Rules*, 2, 74, 103, 220.
37. *De mutatione nominum,* ed. Cohn-Wendland, 157, 166.
38. *De compunctione ad Stelechium* 2.3; PG 47:414 ff.
39. *In ep. ad Hebr.* 15; PG 63:121.
40. PG 48:1055-1059.
41. PG 31:1376 B.
42. *Summa Theologiae* 1a2ae. Q. 60. art. 5. The reference is to Aristotle, *Nicomachean Ethics* 4.8.
43. Cf. W. Heffening, *Die griechische Ephraem–Paraenesis gegen das Lachen in arabischer Übersetzung* (Leipzig, 1927).
44. *In ep. ad Hebr.* 15; PG 63:122.
45. *Paedagogus* 2.5.
46. *In Matth. Comm., sermo* 20.
47. *Oratio* 12.
48. On the true author of this *Doctrina* 24, see OCP (1940)

6:220-221.
49. PG 88:1837 B.
50. *Great Catechesis* 54; ed. Papadopoulo–Kerameus, p. 388.
51. Alph. Agathon 5; Ward, p. 18.
52. Alph. Pambo 13; Ward, p. 166.
53. *Vita S. Euthymii* 52 ff.; Cotelier, 2:243 ff.
54. K. Heussi, *Der Ursprung des Mönchtums*, p. 246 ff.
55. PG 82:1289 C. [Translation forthcoming in the Cistercian Fathers Series. —ed.]
56. *Ibid.*, 1317 A.
57. *Acta Mar Abrahae Kidunaiae* 16; T.J. Lamy, *Sancti Ephraem Syri Hymni et Sermones* (Malines, 1882-1902) 4:48.
58. P. Bedjan, *Acta Martyrum et Sanctorum* (Paris, 1895) 1:370.
59. *Sermo Asceticus;* Ephrem 1:42 ff.
60. *Bibliothek der Kirchenväter, Ephräems ausgewählte Schriften* (Kempten-Munich, 1911-1928) 3:312.
61. *The Precious Pearl* 31; PO 16:674.
62. Nilus, *Epist.* Bk. 2.13; PG 79:205.
63. PG 99:1881B.
64. PG 89:1721-1726.
65. Ammonas, *Instructions* 2.4; PO 11:461 ff.
66. See above, p. 77.
67. PE 2.32, p. 104, Arm. 1, p. 559.
68. PE 2.11, p. 41 ff.
69. PE 2.32, p. 104, Arm. 1, p. 559.
70. Heussi, *Der Ursprung,* pp. 272-275; R. Reitzenstein, *Historia Monachorum und Historia Lausiaca* (Göttingen, 1916) p. 80, note 1.
71. Barsanuphius, letter 466, p. 231.
72. *Centuries* 5.26.
73. *Life of Saint Dositheus,* ed. P.M. Brun, *Orientalia Christiana* 26:120 ff.
74. Alph. Poemen 8; Ward, p. 140 f.
75. See above, p. 55.
76. Alph. Daniel 8; Ward, p. 45.
77. Alph. Copres 3; Ward, p. 101.
78. Alph. Anthony 17; Ward, p. 3 f.
79. *Philoxeni Mabbugensis Tractatus de Trinitate et Incarnatione, Corpus Script. Christ. Orient.* 9-10, ed. G. Vaschalde (Louvain, 1955).
80. Evagrius, *Centuries* 6.37.
81. Barsanuphius, letter 606, p. 292 ff.
82. Letters 607, 608.
83. Letter 609.

84.  Unnumbered letter, p. 295 f.
85.  Letter 612.
86.  Letter 614.
87.  Alph. Sopatros; Ward, p. 189.
88.  A. Boon, *Pachomiana Latina,* pp. 60, 66, n. 7; CS 46:177.
89.  He had entered at the age of 14. Halkin, *Vita Prima* 26, p. 16; CS 45:313.
90.  E. Amélineau, *Histoire de Saint Pachôme et de ses communautés* (Paris, 1889) 1:49 [cf. *Bohairic Life* of Pachomius 30 (CS 45: 55) *First Greek Life* 35 (322)].
91.  *Ibid., The Third Greek Life* 45, p. 280.
92.  *On the Song of Songs* 2; PG 44:784.
93.  *Historia Religiosa* 30; PG 82:1493 AB. Cf. Life of Saint Nicephorus of Miletus, *Analecta Bollandiana* (Brussels, 1896), 14:158.

## CHAPTER VIII

1.  *Adversus Haereses* 6.14, 15.
2.  Alph. Peter the Pionite 2; Ward, p. 168 f.
3.  Alph. Poemen 39; Ward, p. 145.
4.  *De oratione* 48; CS 4:62, translates it as 'to work and to watch'.
5.  PE 2.32, p. 104. Arm 1, p. 559.
6.  *Oratio* 39, 'In sacra Lumina', 17; PG 36:356.
7.  *Oratio* 40.9; col. 369.
8.  *Letter of Bishop Ammon,* 28; Halkin, p. 115; CS 46:97.
9.  Ephrem 5:359-386.
10.  *Ibid.,* p. 364.
11.  PG 47:308.
12.  *De paenitentia* 2.2; PG 49:285.
13.  *Ibid.* 2.3; See also *In Epist. ad Hebr.* 9.
14.  Published by N. Souvarov in *Vizantijskij Vremennik* (1903) 10:55-61.
15.  *De paenit.* 7.5; PG 49:334.
16.  *Ibid.* 7.4; col. 328.
17.  P. Bedjan, *Mar Iacobi Sarugensis Homiliae* (Paris, 1905-10) 2:224.
18.  *Ibid.,* p. 226.
19.  *Ibid.,* p. 227.
20.  Bedjan, p. 315.
21.  *Ibid.,* p. 320

# 194 Penthos

22.  See *Revue d'Ascétique et de Mystique* (1933) 14:171 f.
23.  Theotokis, p. 583.
24.  *Great Catechesis* 27; ed. Papadopoulo–Kerameus, p. 191.
25.  Barsanuphius, letter 76, p. 41; cf. letter 255, p. 140.
26.  See above, pp. 22 f.
27.  Letter 458, p. 227.
28.  PE 2.32, p. 104, Arm. 1, p. 526.
29.  See above, p. 41.
30.  Evagrius, *Antirrheticus,* 'Pride', 21; Frankenberg, p. 540.
31.  *Ibid.,* nos. 5, 6, 13 etc.
32.  Ammonas, *Instructions* 4.14; PO 11:476.
33.  Symeon the New Theologian, 'Practical and Theological Precepts', 68, 69, 74, 75; *Philokalia* (Athens, 1874, 1893) 2:159; ET in Kadloubovsky and G.E.H. Palmer, *Writings from the Philokalia on Prayer of the Heart* (London, 1951) pp. 112, 114 ff.
34.  On this, see 'L'erreur fondamentale et la logique du messalianisme', OCP 1:328 ff., 348 ff.
35.  Chapter 152, *Philokalia* 1.171; cf. *Vie de Syméon,* ed. Hausherr (Rome, 1928), Introduction.
36.  *Vie de Syméon* 90.
37.  See A. Baumstark, *Geschichte der syrischen Literatur* (Bonn, 1922) p. 225 f., and J.B. Chabot, *De S. Isaaci Ninivitae vita, scriptis et doctrina* (Louvain, 1892) p. 63 n. 1, 67 n. 1. [An English translation of the Mystic Discourses and Letters will appear in the Cistercian Studies Series. —ed.]
38.  PG 86:857 C-859 B. Cf. ch. 28.
39.  *Ibid.* 29. The Greek text is in Theotokis, pp. 13 ff. Nicodemus the Hagiorite inserted this text in his collection of catanyctic prayers (pp. 128 ff. See above, p. 15.) Many other texts could be found there. Some are anonymous, some attributed to authors of every age, beginning with Saints Ephrem, Basil and Chrysostom, through John Damascene, Antiochus Pandectes, Simeon Metaphrastes, and Symeon the New Theologian, and ending with Mark Eugenikos and Gennadius Scholarios. Some are translated from Russian, and finally the whole last part (pp. 193-254) is taken from Saint Augustine in the translation of Demetrius Cydones. Nicodemus' principle seems to have been: all that is catanyctic is ours.

## CHAPTER IX

1.  Evagrius, *Praktikos* 2.57; PG 40:1248B; CS 4:32.

2. Cf. Nilus, *De octo spiritibus malitiae* 11, 12; PG 79:1156 C f.
3. Abba Isaiah, ed. Augustinos, (Jerusalem, 1911) logos 16, p. 91.
4. Cf. K. Höll, *Enthusiasmus und Bussgewalt* p. 43 f.
5. *Vie Spirituelle* 48 (1936) [65]-[110].
6. Cf. Alph. Apollo 2; Ward, p. 31.
7. Chap. 153; CS 4:80.
8. Chap. 5, 6, 78; CS 4:56, 68.
9. *In epist. ad Phil.* 14; PG 62:281 f.
10. *Ibid.,* col. 283.
11. *In epist. ad Col.* 12.3; PG 62:384 ff.
12. *Letter* 1:220; PG 79:164.
13. Abba Isaiah, ed. Augustinos, logos 16, p. 90.
14. Ammonas, letter 7.3; PO 11:453. In the translation of Derwas J. Chitty, *The Letters of Ammonas* (Oxford: SLG Press, 1979) p. 18, it is Letter 13.
15. Letter 2.1; PO 11:435; Chitty, Letter 2, p. 2.
16. *Instructions* 4.60; PO 11:480.
17. Ammonas, letter 7.1-2; PO 11.452 ff. The editor, F. Nau, points out that the citation from 'Levi' is absent from the Bible and known apocryphas.
18. Ephrem 1:44 D.
19. *Ibid.,* p. 255 A.
20. See above, p. 17 f.
21. *Centuries* 1.70, 71; PG 120;884.
22. It may be that this Nestorian bishop of Nineveh found his most faithful disciples in the school of the New Theologian. This point deserves a special study which I should like to undertake some day.
23. Wensinck's translation (p. 165) of this word as 'beyond' is not exact. The Greek is ἔσωθεν. The text is dealing with 'natural' contemplation which pierces the materiality of things to seize their 'logos'.
24. Bedjan 35, p. 244 ff; Wensinck, p. 164 ff.
25. PE 2.32, p. 100.
26. The Greek adds: 'and embellish it'.
27. Bedjan, p. 245 ff.
28. Bedjan 14, p. 125-127.
29. Ps 59:5. Maximus, *Expos. in Ps. 59.* 5-7; PG 90:861 C.
30. Barsanuphius, letter 458, p. 227.
31. Letter 81, p. 95.
32. Bedjan 12, p. 122.
33. Bedjan, 40, p. 304. On this division into three stages, see J.B. Chabot, *De S. Isaaci Ninivitae vita,* p. 74.

34.    Bedjan 15, p. 128. Cf. Ezk 47. The Greek has: 'The intellect attains to the vision of signs and revelations such as Ezekiel saw.' The translator has missed the point. The editor Nicephoras adds a long note which tries to explain this by Ezk 1:4, but all this is irrelevant to Isaac's train of thought.

35.    See I. Hausherr, 'Aux origines de la mystique syrienne, Gregoire de Chypre ou Jean de Lycopolis', OCP 4 (1938) 497-520.

36.    See Mk 3:5: a variant from MS Syrus Sinaiticus.

37.    Sven Dedering, *Johannes von Lykopolis, Ein Dialog über die Seele und die Affekte des Menschen* (Leipzig–Uppsala–Haag, 1936) pp. 16-18; French translation by I. Hausherr in *Orientalia Christiana Analecta* 120:40–42.

38.    Hausherr, 'Aux origines . . . ' , Introduction, p. 15 ff.

39.    *Ibid.,* pp. 10, 23.

40.    *Vie de Syméon,* 69-70, pp. 93-97.

41.    *Peri Archon* 2.8; *Centuries* 2.68; 3.40.

42.    'The unattainable here becomes a fact.' Goethe, *Faust.*

43.    Dedering, pp. 85-89; Hausherr, pp. 98-103.

44.    *Epist.* 1.319; PG 78:367.


EPILOGUE

1.    K. Höll, *Enthusiasmus und Bussgewalt,* p. 61.

2.    *Vie de Syméon* 134.

3.    H. Böhmer, *Studien zur Geschichte der Gesellschaft Jesu* (Bonn, 1914) 1:58 ff.

4.    *Adversus Haereses* 4.64.

5.    See his *Sermones adversus Scrutatores.*

6.    *De oratione* 5; CS 4:56 ('rudeness').

7.    In the special number of *Revue Liturgique et Monastique* published for the fourteenth centenary of Monte Cassino (Maredsous, 1929) 338-399.

8.    PE 4.13, p. 60. Arm. 2, p. 208.

9.    *In epist. ad Hebr.* 15; PG 63: 122 ff.

10.    B. Steidle, 'Ein mystisches Problem im alten Mönchtum', *Benediktinische Monatschrift,* 20 (Beuron, 1938) 181-187; L. Gillet in *Sobornost* (1937) 5 ff.; M. Lot–Borodine, 'Le mystère du "don des larmes" dans l'Orient chrétien', *Vie Spirituelle,* 48 (1936) [65]-[110].

11.    Alph. Anthony 8; Ward, p. 2.

12.    Alph. Poemen 164; Ward, p. 159.

13.    F. Nau, in appendix to the Plerophories of John Rufus,

PO 8:104. In the sequel, Abba Isaiah reassures the two visitors of the orthodoxy of Chalcedon.

14.  *Letter* 1.1; PG 52:549 ff.

15.  *Letter* 2.1; col. 556.

16.  *In Epist. ad Cor. I* 38.5; PG 61:329.

17.  Maximus the Confessor, 'Alia Capita ex Vaticano', 57, 58; PG 90:1413 BC.

18.  See above, p. 139.

19.  *De virginitate* 18; ed. E. van der Goltz, *Texte und Untersuchungen* 29 (Leipzig, 1905) 52.

20.  Evagrius, *Exhortatio,* ed. H. Gressmann, *Texte und Untersuchungen* 39 (Leipzig, 1913) 146-151.

21.  *Exhortatio* 25; Gressmann, p. 148.

22.  *De oratione* 7, 8; CS 4:56-7.

23.  'Quod non oporteat ridere,' Ephrem 1:254.

24.  *Great Catechesis* 96; ed. Papadopoulo–Kerameus, p. 692.

25.  *Short Rules* 209; PG 31:1221 C.

26.  *Asceticus* 27-41; PG 90:932 C-952 A.

27.  *De beatitudine* 3; PG 44:1224 C ff.

28.  *Ibid.,* col. 1228 C ff. See Alph. Arsenius 6; Ward, p. 8.

29.  See Nicetas Stethatos, *Centuries* 2.25.

30.  Barsanuphius, letter 17, p. 9 ff.

31.  Evagrius, *Centuries* 3.55.

32.  *Oratio* 57; cf. PG 120:297.

33.  See *Vie de Syméon* 4, p. 7. Diadochus, *De perfectione* 25, 29; ed. Weis-Liebersdorf, p. 27 ff.

34.  Gregory of Nyssa, *De hominis opificio* 12; PG 44:164 C.

35.  See above, p. 11.

36.  Chrysostom, *In S. Paulum* 2; PG 50:481; Basil, *De gratiarum actione;* PG 31:217 B.

37.  Isidore of Pelusium, *Epist.* 2.176; 3.8; PG 78; Basil, *ubi supra.*

38.  Gregory of Nyssa, *De hominis opificio* 12; PG 44:157 D, 160 BC.

39.  Basil, *De gratiarum actione;* Nemesius, *De natura hominis* 20.

40.  *Oratio* 32; PG 120:480 C.

41.  *Oratio funebris de Placilla;* PG 46:880 C.

42.  Nilus, *Letter* 3.257; PG 79:512 ff.

43.  Barsanuphius, letter 18, p. 10 ff. On the coldness of the devil, see the chapter inserted into Evagrius' *Praktikos* 1.66 (PG 40:1240 C), 'The bodies of demons are extremely cold'. See also CS 4:lxxvi.

44.  See above, pp. 26-7.

45.  See *Vie de Syméon,* Introduction, p. xlviii.

46. Ammonas, *Instructions* 4.1; PO 11:474.

47. John Climacus, degree 7; PG 88:816 D.

48. Bedjan 35, p. 252. The Greek version of this passage is cited in PE 2.32, p. 100 with some omissions and variants.

49. PG 120:479-493. This saying is found in the *Book of Simeon Studite,* joined erroneously to the *Capita Moralia* of the New Theologian, PG 120:681A, n. 144.

50. *Ibid.,* col. 473 f., note 13.

51. *Vie de Syméon,* Introduction, p. xl.

52. *In Lucam* 1.

53. Nicephoras, *De custodia cordis;* PG 147:948 A; Gregory Nazianzen, *Oratio in sanctum baptisma;* PG 36:412 C.

54. Irenaeus, *Adversus Haereses* 4.25.

55. PE 2.32, p. 101 f. Arm. 1.550.

56. Alph. Arsenius 46; Ward, p. 16.

57. Alph. Anthony 14; Ward, p. 3. See above, pp. 43-4.

58. *In epist. ad Col.* 12:2; PG 62:383.

59. *Life of St Anthony* 45; PG 26:908 C.

60. *Ibid.* 67; tr. by A. Robertson, in P. Schaff and H. Wace, edd., *A Select Library of Nicene and Post-Nicene Fathers. Second Series* (New York, 1903) 4: *Athanasius,* p. 214.

61. Alph. Anthony 28; Ward, p. 6.

62. Evagrius, *Centuries* 5.39.

# TABLE OF ABBREVIATIONS

Alph.

The Alphabetical Series of the *Apophthegmata Patrum;* PG 65; translated by Benedicta Ward, *The Sayings of the Desert Fathers* (London and Kalamazoo, Michigan, 1975).

Arm.

The Armenian version of the *Apophthegmata;* L. Leloir, ed., *Paterica Armenica; Corpus Scriptorum Christianorum Orientalium* 353: *Subsidia* 42 (Louvain, 1974– ).

Barsanuphius

Βίβλος ψυχωφελεστάτη περιέχουσα ἀποκρίσεις . . . Βαρσανουφίου καὶ Ἰωάννου. Nicodemus the Hagiorite, ed. (Venice, 1816). [Translation projected in the Cistercian Studies Series—ed.]

Bedjan

*Isaac Ninivita, De Perfectione Religiosa* (Paris–Leipzig, 1909).

Cotelier

*Ecclesiae Graecae Monumenta* (Paris, 1677-92).

CS

Cistercian Studies Series (Spencer, Mass., Washington, D.C., Kalamazoo, Mich., 1969– ).

Ephrem

*Sancti Patris Nostri Ephraem Syri Opera Omnia* (Rome, 1732-1746) vv. 1-6.

Frankenburg

W. Frankenburg, *Evagrios Pontikus* (Berlin, 1912).

Halkin

F. Halkin, ed. *Sancti Pachomii Vitae Graecae* (Brussels, 1932). ET by A. W. Athanassakis, *The Life of Pachomius* (Missoula, Montana, 1975) and by Armand Veilleux, *Pachomian Koinonia I: The Life of St Pachomius,* Cistercian Studies Series, 45 (Kalamazoo, 1981).

200                  *Penthos*

OCP            *Orientalia Christiana Periodica* (Rome: Pontificio Istituto per gli Studi Orientali, 1935-  ).

PE               Συναγωνὴ τῶν θεοφθόγγων ῥημάτων καὶ διδασκαλιῶν τῶν . . . πατέρων . . . παρὰ Παύλου . . . τῆς Εὐεργετίδος, (Constantinople, 1861).

PG               J.-P. Migne, *Patrologiae cursus completus, series graeca,* 162 volumes. (Paris, 1857-1866).

PL               J.-P. Migne, *Patrologiae cursus completus, series latina,* 221 volumes (Paris, 1844-1864).

PO               *Patrologia Orientalis* (Paris, 1907-  ).

Theotokis       Τοῦ ὁσίου Πατρὸς ἡμῶν Ἰσαὰκ τοῦ Σύρου τὰ εὑρεθέντα ἀσκητικά, Nicephorus Theotokis, ed. (Leipzig, 1770).

Veilleux        Armand Veilleux, *Pachomian Koinonia,* 3 vols., Cistercian Studies Series, 45, 46, 47 (Kalamazoo, 1981-2).

Vie de Symeon   I. Hausherr, ed., *Vie de Syméon le Nouveau Théologien. Orientalia Christiana,* 12 (Rome: Istituto per gli Studi Orientali, 1928).

VS               *Verba Seniorum;* PL 73 and 74.

Ward           See Alph.

Wensinck     *Mystic Treatises by Isaac of Niniveh, translated from Bedjan's Syriac Text* by A. J. Wensinck (Amsterdam, 1923).

*Psalms have been cited according to the Septuagint-Vulgate enumeration.*

# CISTERCIAN PUBLICATIONS INC.

# TITLES LISTING

## THE CISTERCIAN FATHERS SERIES

## THE CISTERCIAN STUDIES SERIES

*Temporarily out of print      †Forthcoming

*Temporarily out of print* †*Forthcoming*